Discourses in Buddhist Classics

Andhra University Philosophical Studies

1. Life and Teachings of Ādi Śaṅkarācārya; by P. George Victor (ISBN 81-246-0194-1)
2. Saints and Gurus: Perspectives on Spiritual and Social Renaissance in Contemporary India; edited by P. George Victor and S.D.A. Joga Rao (ISBN 81-246-0203-4)
3. Social Relevance of Philosophy: Essays on Applied Philosophy; edited by P. George Victor (ISBN 81-246-0204-2)
4. Teaching Philosophy in the Twenty-First Century; by P. George Victor (ISBN 81-246-0205-0)
5. Studies in Vedānta: Essays in Honour of Professor S.S. Rama Rao Pappu; edited by P. George Victor and V.V.S. Saibaba (ISBN 81-246-0350-2)
6. Discourses in Buddhist Classics; by V.V.S. Saibaba (ISBN 81-246-0360-X)

Andhra University Philosophical Studies, no. 6

Discourses in Buddhist Classics

by

V.V.S. Saibaba

With a Foreword by

Angraj Chaudhary

D.K. Printworld (P) Ltd.

New Delhi

Cataloging in Publication Data — DK
Courtesy: D.K. Agencies (P) Ltd. <docinfo@dkagencies.com>

Saibaba, V.V.S. (Venkata Vadlamani Satya), 1947-
Discourses in Buddhist classics / by V.V.S. Saibaba ; with a foreword by Angraj Chaudhary.
xviii, 166 p. 23 cm. — (Andhra University philosophical studies ; no. 6)
Includes bibliographical references (p.)
Includes index.
ISBN 812460360X

1. Buddhist literature, Pali — History and criticism. 2. Buddhism — Sacred books. I. Title. II. Series: Andhra University philosophical studies ; no. 5.

DDC 294.382 22

ISBN 81-246-0360-X
First published in India in 2006

Published & printed by:
D.K. Printworld (P) Ltd.
Regd. Office: 'Sri Kunj', F-52, Bali Nagar
New Delhi-110 015
Phones: (011) 2545-3975; 2546-6019; *Fax*: (011) 2546-5926
E-mail: dkprintworld@vsnl.net
Website: www.dkprintworld.com

Foreword

THE primary object of this monograph is to describe the basic teachings of the Buddha as enshrined in the Theravāda and Mahāyāna literature. For gleaning materials expounding Theravāda teachings Prof. Saibaba has selected two books viz., the *Dhammapada* a very popular book containing the jewels of ethical teachings, and the *Suttanipāta* — a text regarded as very ancient on the grounds of language and content. The representative texts selected for describing Mahāyāna teachings are the *Saddharmapuṇḍarīka Sūtra* and the *Vajracchedikā Prajñāpāramitā*.

In the first four chapters of the monograph the author tries to prepare the readers for appreciating the Buddha's teachings in their early and developed form. So by way of introducing his teachings the author devotes the first chapter of his book to trace the life of Gautama the Buddha, his teachings as found in the early Buddhist literature and also the object of his teachings based on Pāli and Sanskrit sources. The second chapter is devoted to survey the evolution of Pāli language and literature. The third chapter briefly sketches the three divisions of the Pāli Tipiṭaka viz., the *Vinaya*, the *Sutta* and the *Abhidhamma Piṭaka*s. In the fourth chapter the readers are informed about the fundamental principles of Theravāda; the origins of Mahāyāna Buddhism; how the term Mahāyāna originated and what its salient features are; and the points of agreement and disagreement between Theravāda and Mahāyāna.

Chapter five takes up the four Vaggas from the *Dhammapada* viz., *The Arahanta, the Buddha, the Magga and the Bhikkhu.* In the Arahanta vagga the qualities of an Arhant are brought out in the following *gāthā*:-

santam tassa manaṁ hoti, santā vācā ca kamma ca ।
sammadaññāvimuttassa, upasantassa tādino ॥

i.e. Calm is his mind, calm is his speech, calm is his action, who rightly knowing is wholly freed, perfectly peaceful and equipoised.

In the Buddha vagga the teachings of the Buddha have been beautifully summarized in the following *gāthā*:

sabbapāpassa akaraṇam, kusalassa upasampadā ।
sacittapariyodapanaṁ, etaṁ Buddhānusāsanaṁ ॥

Not to do any evil, to cultivate good, to purify one's mind — this is the Teaching of the Buddhas.

The Magga vagga besides saying that the eightfold path is the best of all paths, four noble truths are the best of truths, non-attachment is the best of states, and the Buddha . . . the all-seeing one is the best of bipeds also contains the quintessence of the Buddha's teachings. When one discerns these with wisdom (*paññā*), then one is disgusted with misery. This is the path to purity.

Because wisdom arises from meditation and wanes without it, so one should conduct oneself in such a way that wisdom may increase.

yogā ve jāyati bhūri, ayogā bhūrisaṅkhayo ।
etaṁ dvedhā patham ñatvā, bhavāya vibhavāya ca ।
tathttānaṁ niveseyya, yathā bhūri pavaḍḍhati ॥

The Buddha makes it clear that everybody has to walk upon the eightfold path and work out his own salvation.

Nobody else, not even he can do it for anybody else. For walking upon the path, purity of three kinds of action is a sine qua non.

In the Bhikkhu vagga restraints of all kinds i.e. restraints in all the sense-organs and restraints in all the three kinds of action are said to be the necessary qualities of a *bhikkhu*. Besides, other qualities of a *bhikkhu* are brought out in this Vagga.

In the second section of chapter five, the author has selected texts from the *Suttanipāta* such as *Khaggavisāṇa Sutta*, *Aṭṭhaka Vagga,* and *Pārāyaṇa Vagga.* The ideals of a Paccekabuddha are described in fortyone powerful stanzas in the *Khaggavisāṇa Sutta*. Each stanza has the refrain "May he wander alone like the horn of a rhinoceros" (*eko care khaggavisāṇakappo*). The ideals of early Buddhism are set forth here in a very lucid but powerful manner. The other two texts selected by the author as representative of Theravāda literature are also very ancient because they along with the *Khaggavisāṇa Sutta* have two commentaries called *Mahā Niddeśa* and *Culla Niddeśa* which are included in the canon itself. Their antiquity is also proved by the fact that they are found in the Chinese Āgamas. Fragments of the Sanskrit version of the two texts have also been found in Eastern Turkestan as said by M. Anesaki. The Aṭṭhaka vagga is mentioned as the *Arthavargiyāni Sūtrāni* in the *Divyāvadāna*. In the Aṭṭhaka vagga also the characteristics of a muni have been enumerated. In the *Paramaṭṭhaka Sutta* it has been asserted that truth is not dependent on any *diṭṭhi* (view) but it transcends all views. How close this view is to the view expressed by the Buddha is explained in the *Brahmajāla Sutta*. The Buddha says there that he knows all the views mentioned here and knows even beyond them but he is not attached to any of them.

tayidaṁ, bhikkhave, Tathāgato pajāanati . . . taṁ ca Tathāgato pajānāti, tato ca uttaritaraṁ ।

pajānāti taṁ ca pajānanaṁ na parāmasati, aparāmasato cassa paccattaññeva nibbuti viditā ॥

The Pārāyana Vagga contains the dialogue between the sixteen disciples of Brāhmaṇa Bāvarī and the Buddha on profound philosophical and sublime ethical subjects. It is clear from these texts that the author has been very careful in selecting them as they are ancient and have enshrined in them the original teachings of the Buddha such as the four noble truths, the eightfold path, and the tilakkhaṇa. One who observes the five precepts (*śila*), practises meditation (*Samādhi*) and attains wisdom (*paññā*) by realizing the true nature of things at the experiential level is bound to end suffering and attain liberation.

In chapter six the texts depicting the salient features of Mahāyāna Buddhism are taken from the *Vajracchedikā Prajñāpāramitā* and the *Saddharmapuṇḍarīkā Sūtra* which are representative texts of Mahāyāna Buddhism. M. Winternitz rightly says that "he who wishes to become acquainted with Mahāyāna Buddhism, with all its characteristic peculiarities, with all its advantages and defects, should read this Sūtra (i.e. the *Saddharmapuṇḍarikā Sūtra*). There is not much of the man Śākyamuni left in this work. The Buddha now is actually nothing less than a God above all gods, an infininitely exalted being who has lived since countless aeons in the past and will live for ever." Here we see the refutation of the early pronouncement of the Buddha that "I won't be born again." Unlike the Buddha of the Pāli canon,the Buddha of the *Lotus Sūtra* speaks just like the Kṛṣṇa of the *Bhāgavad Gītā* and showers compassion on his devotees. The Mahāyāna teachings have been explained through the Parables of *the Saddharma Puṇḍarikā*.

In the *Vajracchedikā Prajñāpāramitā* the Mahāyāna doctrine is at its best. One is just to select only one four-footed verse from the *Vajracchedikā* and explain it to others to acquire greater religious merit than a person who might sacrifice his life day by day for aeons. The tone and tenor of these texts are quite unlike those of the Theravāda texts where men are asked to be pure by driving out all defilements and strive hard for ending their misery. According to these texts, on the other hand, freedom from misery is attained just by reciting the names of the Buddhas and the Bodhisattvas.

The author who has already published three books in the field of Buddhist thought is very well qualified to choose *gāthā*s and suttas from a great mass of literature. He has brought his expertise to bear upon the selection of the Four Texts from Theravāda and Mahāyāna, highlighting their objectives and differences as also bringing out their different aesthetics. This is a very useful monograph for any serious reader who wants to know about Early Buddhism and Mahāyāna. Prof. Saibaba deserves our congratulations and I wish him godspeed in his future academic endeavors.

Buddhapurnima
Dt. 23-05-2005

Angraj Chaudhary
Former Professor of Pali,
Nava Nalanda Mahavihara, Bihar

Dedicated
with profound respect and love
to my father
Shri Venkata Rao, Vadlamani
who has kindled in me
the spark of Bodhicitta

Preface

THE work entitled *Discourses in Buddhist Classics* has been initially undertaken under the Phase-II of U.G.C. Special Assistance Programme in the Department of Philosophy and Religious Studies, Andhra University, Visakhapatnam. It is primarly designed with two-fold objective: (a) To serve as the reading material for Final P.G. Students in the Department, and as the course material for the students of Distance Education who opt for the *Philosophy of The Buddha* as one of their special papers, and (b) To sustain the interest of the enterprising student by providing comprehensive understanding of the themes concerning the syllabi.

The object of the work is to describe the basic teachings of doctrines of Theravāda and Mahāyāna branches of Buddhist philosophy, with the aid of the four representative Buddhist Classical texts, viz. the *dhammapada*, the *Sutta-Nipāta*, the *Vajracchedikā Prajñāpāramitā* and the *Saddharmapuṇḍarīka-Sūtra*. The methodology employed in writing this monograph is mainly textual, analytical and also historical. The material covered in this monograph comprises the Andhra University syllabus prescribed for P.G. (Final) Philosophy students since 1972, introduced by my revered teacher *Padma Vibhushan* K. Satchidananda Murty.

The monograph is divided into six chapters whose contents are as follows:

Chapter 1 seeks to trace the life of Gautama Buddha, based on Pāli and Sanskrit sources; his missionary life depicted in the Pāli canon and the object of his teachings as reflected in the early Buddhist literature;

Chapter 2 surveys the evolution of Pāli language by throwing light on its antiquity; the stages of its development; the significant role of Pāli language and literature as well as the contribution of scholars and institutions to Pāli language and literature.

Chapter 3 provides a brief sketch of the main divisions of the Pāli *Tripiṭaka,* viz. the *Vinaya Piṭaka* the *Sutta Piṭaka* and the *Abhidhamma Piṭaka.*

Chapter 4 (Part 1) elucidates the fundamental principles of Theravāda Buddhism which comprises the sailent features of Theravāda, the doctrines of Dependent Origination, Non-self, Karma and Rebirth, the Four Noble Truths and the Noble Eight-fold Path. Part 2 of Chapter IV comprises the probable origins of Mahāyāna, the evolution of the term "Mahāyāna," its salient features, and the points of agreement and disagreement between Theravāda and Mahāyāna schools.

Chapter 5 (Part 1) furnishes the introduction of the *dhammapada* along with the lucid exposition of the contents in the text namely the Arhant, the Buddha, the Way and the Bhikṣu. Part 2 of Chapter V deals with the main teachings of the *Sutta-Nipāta,* original teachings of the Buddha and also it makes a study of the Buddha's teachings contained in the *Khaggavisāṇa Sutta* (from the *Uraga Vagga*) the "Book of Octades" (*Aṭṭhaka Vagga*) and the "Book of Way-Across" (*Pārāyana Vagga*).

Chapter 6 (Part 1) discusses the Central teachings of the *Vajracchedikā Prajñāpāramitā-Sūtra,* the ideal of Bodhisattva in the Sūtra and the characteristics of the conditioned Phenomena explained through nine similes. Part 2 of Chapter 6 contains an introduction and exposition of the Central teachings of the *Saddharma Puṇḍarīka,* viz. the Ideal of Tathāgata in the *Lotus- Sūtra;* the doctrine of universal salvation; Buddhahood as the highest goal of perfection; the doctrine of Single Vehicle (*Eka-yāna*); the role of Bodhisattvas as Enlighteners and Saviours; the Doctrine of salvation by Faith and Devotion. It also examines the Philosophical significance of the Parables in the *Lotus-Sūtra*.

My deepest debt of gratitude goes to my revered teacher *Padma Vibhushan* K. Satchidananda Murty, a profound scholar of international repute who has not only lectured during the year 1972-73 on the themes covered in this monograph but also with depth of vision promoted Buddhist philosophy by supervising my Ph.D project which enabled me to make an intensive study of the Buddhist classical texts, dealt in this work. My special thanks are due to P. George Victor, Co-ordinator, UGC–Special Assistance Programme, Department of Philosophy for his keen interest and constant persuasion without which this work would never have been completed.

I am indebted to Angraj Chaudhary, Nava Nalanda Mahāvihara for writing a foreword to this book. I deeply appreciate my sons V.S.V.S. Murthy, Vijaya Manjusri Maitreya and Shri P. Kishore Kumar, Dept. of Philosophy, Andhra University for all their valuable assistance and spirit of co-operation in computerising the monograph without which this work would not have been brought to this state of completion. I gratefully acknowledge the generous service rendered by Shri Susheel K. Mittal of D.K. Printworld (P) Ltd., New Delhi for bringing out this book under the series of Andhra University Philosophical Studies.

Visakhapatnam. ***V.V.S. Saibaba***
21 Nov. 2005. Andhra University

Contents

Key to Transliteration

VOWELS

अ *a*	आ *ā*	इ *i*	ई *ī*	उ *u*	ऊ *ū*
(but)	(palm)	(it)	(beet)	(put)	(pool)
ऋ *ṛ*	ए *e*	ऐ *ai*	ओ *o*	औ *au*	
(rhythm)	(play)	(air)	(toe)	(loud)	

CONSONANTS

Guttural	क *ka*	ख* *kha*	ग *ga*	घ *gha*	ङ *ṅa*
	(skate)	(blockhead)	(gate)	(ghost)	(sing)
Palatal	च *ca*	छ* *cha*	ज *ja*	झ *jha*	ञ *ña*
	(chunk)	(catch him)	(john)	(hedgehog)	(bunch)
Cerebral	ट *ṭa*	ठ* *ṭha*	ड *ḍa*	ढ* *ḍha*	ण* *ṇa*
	(start)	(anthill)	(dart)	(godhead)	(under)
Dental	त *ta*	थ *tha*	द *da*	ध* *dha*	न *na*
	(path)	(thunder)	(that)	(breathe)	(numb)
Labial	प *pa*	फ* *pha*	ब *ba*	भ *bha*	म *ma*
	(spin)	(philosophy)	(bin)	(abhor)	(much)
Semi-	य *ya*	र *ra*	ल *la*	व *va*	
vowels	(young)	(drama)	(luck)	(vile)	
Sibilants	श *śa*	ष *ṣa*	स *sa*	ह *ha*	
	(shove)	(bushel)	(so)	(hum)	
Others	क्ष *kṣa*	त्र *tra*	ज्ञ *jña*	ळ* *ḷ*	ॠ* *ṝ*
		(*kṣatriya*)	(*triśūla*)	(*jñānī*)	(*play*)

अं (∸)*ṁ anusvāra* (nasalisation of preceding vowel) like *saṁskṛti*

अः *visarga* = *ḥ* (aspiration of preceding vowel) like (*prātaḥ*)

ऽ *Avagraha* consonant #'consonant (like:- *ime 'vasthitā*)

Anusvāra at the end of a line is presented by m (म्) and not ṁ

HINDI LETTERS (extras)

ँ = *ñ*	∸ = ṅ	ड़ = *ṛa*	ढ़ = *ṛha*
(*candrabindu*)	(*anusvāra*)		

* No exact English equivalents for these letters.

1

Life and Mission of Gautama Buddha

Life of the Buddha

During the span of about a century, we come across a number of studies on the life history of the Buddha by scholars from different parts of the world such as W.W. Rockhill, S. Beal, T.W. Rhys Davids, K.J. Saunders, E.J. Thomas, H. Oldenberg, Alexander Cosma De Koros, A. Foucher, Andre Bareau and Hajime Nakamura. Hajime Nakamura in his encyclopaedic work on *Indian Buddhism*[1] refers to several studies made during the first half of the twentieth century by several Japanese scholars like Tetsujiro Inouye and Kentoku Hori, Chizen Akanuma, Yensho Kanakura, Fumio Masutani, Kogen Mizuno, and H. Nakamura. Based on the results of recent critical textual studies, H. Nakumara wrote a Buddha's biography[2] in which events in Buddha's life were explained with reference to non-Buddhist materials and in the light of the social background as well as archaeological findings.

Even though a complete biography of Gautama Buddha is not found in the Pāli canon, some suttas[3] in the five Nikāyas

1. H. Nakamura, *Indian Buddhism*, A survey with Bibliographical Notes, p. 16, fn.1.
2. *Ibid.*, p. 17.
3. S.R. Goyal, *A History of Indian Buddhism*, p. 108.

of the *Sutta Piṭaka*, viz. The *Mahāpadāna*, the *Sampasādanīya*, the *Mahāparinibbāna* and *Saṅgīti Sutta*s of the *Dīgha Nikāya*, the *Ariyapariyesana*, the *Mahāsaccaka*, the *Bodhirājakumāra* and the *Saṅgārava Sutta*s of the *Majjhima Nikāya*, the *Sutta-Nipāta*, the *Buddha Vaṁsa*, the *Milindapañha* and the *Jātaka*s of the *Khuddaka Nikāya* and *Jātaka Nidāna* provide us incidental references which throw some light on the personality and events of Gautama Buddha's life. According to Buddhist historians, like Rockhill, an early form of Sanskrit tradition contains the Buddha's life in the *Vinaya* of Tibetan scriptures. Among the hybrid Sanskrit sources, the *Mahāvastu* contains a legend of Buddha's biography. The *Lalitavistara*, which originally belongs to the Sarvāstivādin literature, but later was included in the *Vaipulaya-Sūtra* group, provides us a continuous narrative of Buddha's life. Aśvaghoṣa's *Buddha-carita* and the *Abhinishkrama-Sūtra*, which is extant only in Chinese translation, deal with Buddha's early life.

Gautama Buddha (BC 566-486) was born as a Śākya prince in the city of Kapilavastu, which is located, according to researches[4] of archaeologists, either at Tilaurakot in modern Padaria or at Piprahwa. Both Sanskrit and Pāli accounts referred to above state that at the request of gods in Tuṣita heaven to descend on earth the Bodhisattva or the future Buddha looked and decided upon the time, place, country, class, race and parents fit for his birth. According to Sanskrit and Pāli literary sources as well as Indian History, his father was King Suddhodana and his mother Mahā Māya and his childhood name was Siddhārtha.

According to some of the above Nikāya accounts,[5] the future Buddha descended from Tuṣita heaven being quite

4. H. Nakamura, *op. cit.*, p. 18.

5. See. *Mahāpadāna Sutta* (D.N. II), *Acchariyabbhuta dhamma Sutta* (M.N. III), *Jātaka Nidāna Commentary.*

mindful and conscious entered his mother's womb when she was observing celibacy. The *Sampasādanīya* and *Saṅgīti Sutttas* of the *Dīgha Nikāya*[6] and the *Jātaka* commentary inform us that the future Buddha was born with every mental faculty alert, quite undefiled and unstainted. His birth was never regarded as an accidental occurrence. The *Buddhavaṁsa* traces the past lives of Gautama Buddha right from his initial vow aspiring to become a future Buddha. Some Suttas of the *Dīgha,* the *Majjhima,* and the *Aṅguttara Nikāyas* which deal in detail with the conception, the uterine life and Bodhisattva's birth show that his birth is an incarnation by his own wish (aupapāduka) and corroborating this conception the *Milindapañha* describes his birth as 'Parthenogenetic.' The entire life of Gautama Buddha was according to a fixed pattern, which was conforming to minor variations to the life history of other Buddhas. Accordingly on the seventh day after his birth, on his mother's passing away, Siddhārtha Gautama was brought up by his mother's sister (mātuccha) Mahāpajāpati Gotami who is mentioned at several places in the *Vinaya* and *Pāli Nikāyas*. According to Sanskrit Buddhist legendary accounts sage Asita, a great ascetic who by his divine sight learnt about the birth of the Great Being, came by sky to Kapilavastu and prophecied that the child would be the great preacher of *dhamma* and lamented that by such time the ascetic would not live to hear the law. The panel of court astrologers comprised eight brāhmaṇas out of which seven foretold that the child would become either a 'universal king' or a 'Buddha' and the eighth one confirmed that the infant would become only a Buddha. Due to this prophecy King Suddhodana did his best in keeping his growing son always amidst pleasure and pomp and got him married to lady Yasodhara (also differently named in different literary sources as Bhadda, Subhaddaka, Bimba).

---

6. See. *Dīgha Nikāya,* XXVIII, XXXIII Suttas.

According to the accounts of Mahāvagga of the *Sutta-Nipāta* and the *Nidāna kathā,* Siddhārtha was blessed with a son named Rāhula.

By the sight of four omens, viz. three signs of suffering: old age, disease and death, and an ascetic retired (*pabbajitam*) from worldly life he became aware of the crises of life. Having reflected over these subjects, he lost pride of youth, the royal pomposity and sumptuous life he led as the Crown Prince at the royal court. Obsessed with the problems of human life, he retired from household life at the age of twenty-nine in search of ultimate deliverance from human suffering by secretly leaving his palace and became a recluse.

According to Sanskrit Buddhist sources such as the *Lalitavistara,* after his great renunciation, he was persuaded by the officials of his father's court to return to his kingdom, but in vain.

During his wanderings he met two great ascetic-teachers namely Alara (Arada) Kalama and Rudraka Rāmaputra who were probably dwelling near Vaisali in the Vajjian country. They taught him the seventh and eighth stages of meditation (*Samapatti*) respectively known as the "realm of nothingness" (*ākiñcaññāyatana*) in which one's mind seeks nothing, and "the realm of neither consciousness nor yet non-consciousness" (*n'evasaññā nāsaññā yatana*) in which the sense perception was neither active nor dead. Having mastered these techniques of meditation in a very short time, Gautama found that they do not lead to peace (*nibbānaya*). Despite these teachers' wish to stay and lead their disciples, Gautama left them as their systems of meditation, which aim to attain the states of "Non-existence and Thoughtless Thought" were not the ways to enlightenment (*nayam maggo bodhiya ti*). At Gayasīrsha hill he found a number of ascetics who were indulging in rigorous practices of self-mortification for spiritual elevation. Having observed that they are far from the goal of true insight and knowledge Gautama abandoned them.

Gautama went to Uruvela and practised rigorous asceticism for six long years in the company of the five recluses (*pañca pabbajita*), viz. Kondanna, Vappa, Bhaddiya, Mahānāma and Assaji. Having realised that it would not lead to perfect knowledge and it is not the true way to enlightenment, leaving them he went to General's township at Uruvela on the bank of the Nerañjara River. There he took rice-milk (*khīra*) offered by Sujata the daughter of local Senani who mistook him as the spirit of banyan tree (*nigrodha-rukkha*).

Siddhārdha Gautama sat with a determination not to leave the seat of *vajrāsana* under the Bodhi tree till he attains Sambodhi. Māra the god of desire tried in vain to obstruct Gautama's efforts to enlightenment firstly by frightening him through his host of demons, etc., and secondly by the allurement of his three daughters, Taṇhā, Rati and Rāga who symbolize human passions. After defeating the Māra's army by sun-set he gradually rose from the first to the fourth Jhāna during the three watches of the night, Gautama Sākyamuni acquired the three knowledges of (i) previous existences, (ii) divine vision and (iii) the causative process, and by attaining omniscience (*sabbannuta-nāṇam*) he became the Samyak Sambuddha.

After attaining enlightenment the Buddha remained for four to seven weeks contemplating on the constituents of enlightenment while enjoying *vimutti sukha*. The Mahā Vagga of the *Vinaya Piṭaka* narrates the visit of two merchants Tapussa and Bhalluka from Uṭkala who took twin-refuge (*dvi-saraṇā*) under him.[7]

---

7. T.W. Rhys Davids and H. Olden bers, *Vinaya texts*, Part I, pp. 83-84. see. *The Mahāvagga*, I Khandaka.

In view of the nature of the truth realised by him, which was too deep and subtle to comprehend by people of ordinary intellect, the Buddha hesitated to preach the contents of the wisdom, but being persuaded by Brahma Sahampati, he decided to teach the *dhamma* in the world for all those who have faith to hear it.[8] Intending to teach the *dhamma* to his two former ascetic teachers, he found by his divine sight that they had expired. Hence he went to Sarnath at Varanasi and preached his first sermon (known as the *dhamma-cakka-pavattana sutta*) to his five former brāhmaṇa ascetic companions. At the end of his discourses on the fifth day when he pronounced discourse on the absence of signs of permanent individual self (*Anattā-lakkhaṇa sutta*) all the five elders had become *arahats*.

Buddha's Missionary Life

The Buddha's missionary activities extended from his thirty-fifth year and uninterruptedly continued for about forty-five years, i.e., till the end of his life. He started his missionary activity at Sarnath where by turning the Wheel of Law for the first time (*pāṭhama dhāmmacakka pavattana*) he imparted his teachings to his five former companions mentioned above. Rājagṛha, Srāvasti and Vaisāli were the main centres of Buddha's missionary activities.

Among the disciples of the Buddha, Sāriputta and Mahā-Moggallana, who were formerly the disciples of Sañjaya the sceptic, after their conversion became top-most disciples. Mahā Kāccayāna assumed the greatest role in the history of early Buddhist missions. Ānanda, a favourite disciple of Gautama supported the progressives or liberals. During his missionary life the prominent personalities of diverse walks of life

8. *Ibid.*, p. 88, *Vinaya* I. I. 5,12.

accepted the Buddha *dharma*. They included kings like Pāsenadi, Bimbisāra, Ajātaśatru, Suddhodana, Rāhula, Siddhārtha's son, youths of Śākyan families like Ānanda, Anuruddha, Bhaddīya, Kimbila, Nanda and Devadatta, learned members of influential brāhmaṇa class such as Jānussoni, Aggika Bharadwaja, Kūtadanta, Dhanañjani, Pokkarasādi, Lohiccha, Chaṅki, Vakkali, Bāvari a royal priest of king of Kośala, Anādhapiṇḍaka and lady Visākhā from Setthi class, Chaṇḍaka the attendent and charioteer of Siddhārtha, Ājīvikas like Vekhanassa and Potthapāda, Niganthas like Sīha a Licchavi, general Dabba Mallaputta and Chunda Kamāraputta among Mallas. Jīvaka a renowned physician, Jyotishka son of a fabulously rich banker of Rājagaha, Srona Kotivisa son of a rich banker of Champa, Upāli of a barber's family, Jātila ascetics like Keniya and Sela, Aṅgulīmāla a dacoit son of the priest of King Prasenajit took refuge in the Buddha. Besides the above, prominent ladies who adhered to the Buddha-dharma include Mahāprajāpati Gotami, queen Visākhā, Khema the queen of Bimbisāra and Queen Mallikā of Kośala.

The Buddha's hint to Ānanda to beg him to remain during the aeon in the Cāpāla shrine during his sojourn in Vaisali could not be followed by Ānanda whose heart was possessed by Māra. As a consequence of his promise to Māra that at the end of three months he would attain parinibbāna, according to Pāli tradition, the Buddha is said to have deliberately rejected the rest of his natural term of life. After completing his mission of propagating the law (*dhamma*) for forty-five years and organising the monastic order (*saṅgha*), owing to the food offered by Chunda a blacksmith of Pāvā the Buddha fell ill suffering from indigestion. On the full-moon day of Vaisākha, at the age of eighty he entered into Parinirvāṇa at Kusinagara among the Mallas.

Mission of the Buddha

According to Karl Jaspers,[9] Buddha is one of the four "paradigmatic" individuals, the other three being Socrates, Confucius and Jesus who became the foundations of powerful philosophical movements. In his view Buddha's knowledge is foreign to the world. His mission is self-redemption from suffering. Redemption by insight is the core of his teaching. Redemption lies in right knowledge. The sole objective of his preaching *dhamma* is to obtain self-salvation by the elimination of suffering and to achieve spiritual progress. He diverted the attention of mankind from the belief in Creator God and gods towards the complete cessation of suffering. Christmas Humphreys points out that the task of the Buddha was to reform the corrupt form of Brāhmaṇism, the prevailing religion of his time.

The Buddha maintained silence on metaphysical questions like "God" and "Supernatural" because of three reasons, viz. (i) They are ethically unimportant, (ii) They are irrelevant to the major problems of suffering, (iii) Metaphysical issues like the origin and destruction of cosmos, the eternity and non-eternality of the self, etc., are unprofitable and ineffectual on the path to comprehend the truth and to put an end to the evil of suffering.

Scholars like Christmas Humphreys think[10] that there is no measure of certainty regarding the identification of original message of the Buddha. While attempting to elucidate the true purpose of the Buddha's teachings, Hajime Nakamura distinguishes original Buddhism from early Buddhism.[11]

---

9. Karl Jaspers, *The Great Philosophers*, see, Introduction, pp. 6-7.
10. Christmas Humphreys, *Buddhism*, p. 13.
11. H. Nakamura, *op. cit.*, p.57.

According to him, the peculiarly Buddhistic ideas of original Buddhism[12] seem to be:

(i) The term "Buddha" was used to both Jain sages who have attained enlightenment and non-Jain sages, viz. Upaniṣad philosophers, such as Uddālaka and Yājñavalkya. For instance in the earliest Buddhist works like the *Sutta-Nipāta* the word 'Buddha' connotes "an excellent ascetic" and not the glorified and deified Buddha.

(ii) Even though Gautama was looked upon as an excellent personage he was not deified in the original Buddhism.

(iii) Buddhist recluses similar to the hermits of the Indian epics lived in solitude but not in monasteries. The life of Buddhist ascetics in its incipient stage was fairly different from the monastic life of monks.

(iv) Nuns did not exist in the earliest stage of Buddhism.

(v) At the time of the composition of the earlier Gāthās the fully developed form of Buddhist disciplines (*Pāṭimokkha*) did not exist.

(vi) Buddha refuted dogmas (*diṭṭhi*) of other religious and philosophical schools.

As distinct from the above, H. Nakamura thinks[13] that the early Buddhist ideas are as follows:

(i) The principal ideas of early Buddhism are 'Anicca,' 'dukkha' and 'Anatta.'

(ii) *Dhamma* is the central conception of Buddhism; Buddha is one who sees *dhamma*.

---

12. *Ibid.*, pp. 57-60.

13. *Ibid.*, pp. 61-71.

(iii) Suffering is the fundamental problem of early Buddhism.

(iv) The ultimate purpose of the teaching of the non-self is to get rid of selfish desires; it is nothing except 'enlightenment.'

(v) Buddhism aimed at establishing the existential subjectivity or individuality by the negation of the ego, which can be found in none of the five groups of existence, viz. Corporeality (*rūpa*), feeling (*vedanā*), perception (*saññā*), mental formation (*saṅkhāra*) and consciousness (*viññāṇa*).

(vi) The first sermon, which was conceived with the four noble truths and the "middle way," was the first systematised teaching of the Buddha. The teaching of the middle way (majjhima paṭipadā) is the basis of early Buddhist Ethics which aimed at freedom from the two extremes of activism and hedonism.

(vii) The doctrine of causation, viz. the law of dependent origination (paṭicca samuppāda) discovered by him during his meditation is taught as the key to attain the goal of *nirvāṇa*. The dynamic structure of the concept of dependent origination reveals also the inner working of our mind through which human conversion from ignorance (avijjā) to enlightenment becomes possible.

(viii) *Nirvāṇa* is not only absolute nothingness but also "perfect peace," deliverance (*mokṣa*) or freedom.

(ix) Several Mahāyāna ideas such as Sunna, Viññāṇa Cittamātra are found in Pāli texts in their embryonic form.

(x) Thus early Buddhism inherited many of the Āryan traditional elements, it owed a great deal to

Brāhmaṇism, Upaniṣadic thought and also non-Brāhmaṇic religions such as Ājīvikas and Jains.

Whereas scholars like Nakamura opine that Buddhism did not proclaim a unified or consecutive doctrine and the teachings could differently be understood depending upon the mental calibre of the hearers, others like Karl Jaspers[14] hold that Buddha is a type rather than a 'personality' and he teaches "a path of salvation" which is itself termed "as a form of pedagogic system."[15] That is why perhaps Zimmer[16] hailed Buddhism by classifying it as one of the "five philosophies of Eternity," the other four being Brāhmaṇism, Sāṅkhya, Jainism and Tantra. This is perhaps because as Christmas Humphreys rightly observes:

> The Buddha's enlightenment is the womb, the heart and raison d'etre of Buddhism. It is the criterion of all Buddhist teaching that it conduces or does not conduce to the achievement of enlightenment.[17]

---

14. Karl Jaspers, *op. cit.*, p. 44.
15. *Ibid.*, p. 36.
16. Heinrich Zimmer, *Philosophies of India*, see Part III.
17. Christmas Humphreys, *op. cit.*, p. 15.

2

Origin and Development of the Pāli Language

Definitions of the word "Pāli"

The Pāli lexicons by R.C. Childers[1] as well as T.W. Rhys Davids and W. Stede[2] render the word Pāli into English which originally meant "a line, row, a causeway, bridge and bank." It is further translated as a "norm" or the canon of Buddhist writings or a sacred text: the text of the Pāli canon. Thus the word Pāli was employed figuratively by the Buddhists to mean "a text" or a passage from their sacred texts, which are rehearsed and fixed in three Buddhist councils. Here Pāli refers to specifically the original text of "Tipiṭaka" in contrast with commentary ("Pāliyan" as opposed to "Aṭṭhakathayan").[3] According to Childers,[4] Pāli is also meant a series of texts of various lengths. The *Abhidhānappadīpikā*[5] by Moggalana composed around 12 *c.* CE regards "Tanti" Buddha-Vacana

1. R.C. Childers, *A Dictionary of the Pāli Languages*, Hereafter abbreviated as *DPL*, p. 321.
2. T.W. Rhys Davids and William Stede, *Pāli-English Dictionary*, Hereafter abbreviated as *PED*, p. 455.
3. *Ibid.*
4. Supra.1.
5. Bharat Sinh Upadhyay, *Pāli Sāhitya Kā Itihāsh*, pp. 8-9.

and "Paṅkti" as synonyms of Pāli. One of the Pāli lexicons[6] further defines: as it Preserves the Buddha-vacana in the form of the sacred texts it is called Pāli. (*po pāleti, rakkhati ti Pāli*). According to another connotation, during 1st or 2 *c.* CE Pāli is understood as the text, which protects the sense of the words. (*saddattham pāleti-ti Pāli*).[7]

Date and Antiquity of the Pāli Language

According to the internal textual evidence, the Buddha called his teachings by the word *dhammavinaya* only and does not seem to have used the word Pāli anywhere. For instance the commentary on the *Brahmajāla sutta* states:

(a) "Let the doctrine I have preached you, the discipline I have prescribed for you, be your teacher when I am gone" (*yo vo ānando mayā "dhammo ca vinayo ca desito. paññatto so vo mam accayana satthi*).

(b) In the same work it is stated at another place. "Now we would make a recension of the doctrine and discipline" (*idāni dhammavinaya saṅgahaṁ karoma*).

The term "Pāli" was used for the first time in the commentaries on the Tipiṭaka of Ācārya Buddhaghoṣa (4-5 *c.* CE). We do not find the usage of the term in any earlier Buddhist writings except in Buddhaghoṣa's *Sumaṅgala Vilāsinī* (Dīgha Nikāya commy.), *Aṭṭhasālini* (Dhammasaṅganī commy) *Puggalapaññatti Aṭṭhakathā* on the Abhidhamma works, commentarial works and also in his *Visuddhimagga*. Buddhaghoṣa uses the word in two senses:[8] (a) Buddha-vacana or original texts of *Tripiṭaka*. (b) Textual portions of *Tripiṭaka*.

6. Ācārya, Buddharakshita, *Concise Pāli Course*, Parts I & II, See Preface.
7. D.L. Barua, *Elements of Pāli Grammar*, See Preface, p. iv.
8. Bharat Singh Upadhyay, *op. cit.*, p. 1.

In the Ceylonese chronicles, viz. the *Dīpavaṁsa* composed in 4 *c.* CE and the *Cūla vaṁsa*, composed in 13 *c.* CE Pāli was used respectively to denote Buddha-vacana and original Buddhist texts as distinguished from the commentaries. Ācarya Dharmapāla (5-6 *c.* CE) the other famous commentator in his *Paramaṭṭha-Dīpani* (*Khuddaka Nikāya* commentary) defined Pāli in the sense of original canonical texts. In this context the *Mahāvaṁsa* provides some important references according to which "Pāli" is meant only the original *Tripiṭaka*.

(i) The commentary on the *Samannaphala Sutta* of the *Dīgha Nikāya* states "is to be found neither in the text nor in the commentary" (*neva pāliyaṁ na aṭṭhakathāyam dissati*).

(ii) According to the *Mahāvaṁsa*, 207 "the text of the *Tripiṭaka* and its commentary" (*piṭakattayapāliñ ca tassā aṭṭhakathān ca*).

(iii) The text alone was brought here, we have not got the commentaries *pālimattam idhanitam n'atthi aṭṭhakathā idha*.

(iv) In the same works *Mahāvaṁsa* 252 "In the three versions there was not the slightest variation from the Theravādins, from the texts of the scriptures, from the words or from the letters" (*theravādehi pālehi padehi vyanjanehi ca aññatthattam ahu n'eva potthakesu pi tisu pi*).

(v) In the *Mahāvaṁsa*, 253, it is said that it held the commentary in the same estimation as the text (*pālim viya tam aggahuṁ*).

Theories on the Evolution of the Word "Pāli"

Linguistic experts in their search for the original form of the word "Pāli" set forth the three following theories: In

Saddhamma Saṅgaha composed by Saddhanand in 14 *c.* CE Pāli is used in the above sense only.

(a) We find the earlier form of "Pāli" in the word "*Paryāya,*" which occurs many times in the *Tripiṭaka* sometimes associated with the word *dhamma* and also "alone." The word *Paryāya* refers only to the Buddha's teachings. Later the perverted form of *Pariyāya,* i.e., *Pāliyāya* came into existence. For instance in the Ashokan Bhabru Edict the "word" *Pāliyāya* is used in the sense of *Pariyaya.* In course of time the word *Pāliyāya* was used in the abbreviated form as "Pāli" which denotes Buddha-vacana or original *Tripiṭaka.* This theory was put forward by Bhikshu Jagadish Kashyap.[9]

(b) According to the second theory set forth by Siddhārtha, the Sanskrit word "Pāth" (Pat) is the root of "Pāli." The perverted from of Path is "Pāli." According to this interpretation, the Path of Vedic Saṁhitās was used by brāhmaṇa scholars in the sense of "Pāli" which later was transformed into "Pāli."[10]

(c) According to the third theory put forward by Pandit Vidhusekhar Bhattacharya[11] "Pāli," means, "Paṅkthi" which had undergone a gradual transformation into Patti, Pālli and finally "Pāli."

Besides, there are others such as C. Humphreys who maintain that the word "Pāli" originates from Prākṛt, which gradually transformed into Pākat, Pāvad, Pāval and finally into Pāli. While acknowledging the significant contribution of

---

9. Bhikshu Jagadish Kashyap, *Pāli Mahāvyākaran,* pp. 8-12.
10. Bharat Singh Upadhyay, *op. cit.,* p. 5.
11. *Ibid.,* p. 7.

most of Japanese scholars, Hajime Nakumara concludes that Pāli is a sort of Prākṛt.[12]

Today "Pāli" means that language which preserves Theravāda Buddhist literature that is extant now. As regards the date of Pāli, it was a literary speech, which belongs to the early Middle Indo-Āryan period, the old Indo-Āryan period being represented by the Vedic. Chronologically, Pāli stands midway between the Vedic on the one hand and Sanskrit and the literary Prākṛts on the other. It preserves a number of Vedic traits, which are absent in Sanskrit. The valuable data furnished by Pāli scholars shows the process of its change from the Vedic to Sanskrit and that of the formation of various literary Prākṛts. According to R.C. Childers,[13] "Pāli" as a name for Buddhist scriptures was of late introduction probably dating from 1st or 2 *c.* CE. B.C. Law also contends[14] that the term "Pāli language" is comparatively a modern coinage which was not recognised as a "nomenclature" for any kind of language up to 6th or 7 *c.* CE.

As regards the nature and characteristics of the original language wherein the Buddha's utterances have been preserved it is traditionally believed by Ācārya Buddhaghoṣa as well as noted Grammarians of Pāli and the Ceylonese chronicles that Māgadhi was the medium of expression of the Buddha. For example Buddhaghoṣa in his *Samantapāsādikā* the *Vinaya* commentary affirms Māgadhi as "the language used by the Supremely Enlightened one" (*sammāsambuddhena vuttapakāro māgadhako voharo*). Noted Grammarian Kāccayāna in his *Kāccayāna Vyākaraṇam* expresses that Māgadhi itself is the original language in which Samyak Sambuddha spoke (*sā*

12. H. Nakamura, *op. cit.*, p. 22.

13. *DPL*, p. 322.

14. Bimala Churn Law, *A History of Pāli Literature*, see Introduction. p. ix.

māgadhi mūlabhāsa. . . sambuddha cāpi bhāsare). Moggalana Mahāthera who lived in Sri Lanka during the second half of 12 *c.* CE begins his Pāli Grammar, with these words:

bhacissam māgadhi saddha lakkhaṇam.

I will tell the characteristics of Māgadhi

Similarly the *Cūlavaṁsa* of 13th *c.* CE records the instruction of Bhadant Revata to Buddhaghoṣa to visit Sri Lanka in order to translate Buddhist commentaries from Ceylonese into Pāli as follows:

māgadhanām niruttiya, parivattehi.

Views of Scholars on the Original Home of Pāli Language

Noted scholars on Pāli language and literature widely differ on the issue of the probable origin and home of Pāli.[15]

(a) Rhys Davids opines that Kośala was the home of Pāli based on his hypothesis that it was spoken during 6 *c.* BC in Kośala and the Buddha might have delivered his teachings in his mother tongue.

(b) Westergard and Kuhn hold that Ujjayani was the birth place of Pāli because it has great similarities with Aśokan inscriptions of Girnar and as the Ujjayani dialect was the mother tongue of Mahendra who propagated Sthaviravāda in Sri Lanka.

(c) R.O. Franke, Stenknow and Nalinaksha Dutt traced the central and western parts of Vindhya as the original home of Pāli because of its great similarity with Girnar inscription and with Paisāci Prākṛt, which was spoken around Ujjayani in Vindhya.

15. Bharat Singh Upadhyay, *op. cit.*, pp. 13-22.

(d) H. Oldenberg and E. Müller contend that the original home of Pāli was Kaliṅga because Buddhadharma spread from there to Sri Lanka its neighbouring country.

(e) Luders affirms that old Ardha-Māgadhi was the foundation of Pāli based on his hypothesis that the original *Tripiṭaka* was in Ardhamāgadhi which was translated later based on Western dialect.

(f) Max Walleser endeavours to explain Pāli as the language of Paṭaliputra.

(g) Scholars like Ryusho Hikata, Ernest Waldschmidt, F. Edgerton unanimously hold that the Buddha probably used several languages for spreading his teachings.

(h) The studies of Indian and Japanese scholars namely P.C. Bagchi, Egaku Maeda and Meiji Yamada indicate that North Western India is the native place of Pāli and the people there adopted it on the advent of Buddhism.

(i) A host of scholars like James Alwis, Childers, E. Conze, Windsch, S. Levi, Winternitz, Grierson, Clough, Geiger, G.D. Bond and Indians like Bhikshu Jagadish Kashyap, Rāhul Sankrityayan and Siddhārtha unanimously agree that, a kind of Māgadhi is the basis of "Pāli."

(j) James Alwis thinks that Pāli the language of the Magadha was one of the sixteen dialects prevalent in India when Buddhism arose. According to him, when Theravāda Buddhist scriptures were written preference was given to Māgadhi.

(k) R.C. Childers contends on the basis of internal evidence that the vernacular of the people was Pāli whose geographical name is Māgadhi which has two or three dialects.

(l) Edward Conze asserts that Pāli was a West Indian dialect and it was not a medium of speech of the Buddha who spoke some kind of Māgadhi, which is lost to us.

(m) Sylvan Levi a reputed French Buddhist scholar speculates that the Buddha-vacana was originally in early Māgadhi, which was translated into Pāli.

(n) Winternitz speculates that like other literary languages Pāli had sprung from an admixture of several dialects employed by the Buddhists wherein Māgadhi was the chief. Since Pāli was the chosen dialect as a compromise among others when Theravāda canon was systematised during post-Aśokan period when Buddhism had spread throughout the whole Central and Northwestern India, it bears similarities of many Indo-Āryan dialects.

(o) Grierson also agrees that Māgadhi was the basis of Pāli based on his argument that a form of Māgadhi was spoken in Taxsila University wherein the early *Tripiṭaka* was compiled.

(p) Clough elucidates the word "Pāli" as a name of the "Magadha Bhāṣā," which is the ancient language of South Bihar.

(q) G.D. Bond remarks that one who attempts to retrace the original Buddhist canon will recognise that similar to Sanskrit, Pāli language is closely related to Māgadhi.

(r) According to Paṇḍit Rāhul Sankrityayan, a great historian and Indologist who made an excellent contribution to Buddhist and Marxist philosophies, some Gujarāti immigrants in Ceylon fundamentally wrote the *Tripiṭaka* in Māgadhi but during the process of its memorisation for a span of two and half centuries, the characteristics of Māgadhi had become extinct in it.

(s) Agreeing with the above scholarly opinion Wielhelm Geiger makes a laudable attempt in order to establish Māgadhi as the basis of Pāli from the viewpoints of both language and content. His substantial scholarly arguments have been summarised as follows:[16] Geiger thinks that Pāli is not pure Māgadhi, but was a form of popular speech, which was based on the Māgadhi that was in existence in pre-Buddhistic times in India. For fulfilling the need of intercommunication natives of Magadh, Kośala, Avanti and other regions used to speak this common inter regional language differently. Even though the Buddha does not belong to Magadh since most of his life was spent there it is natural that there could have been a strong impact of Māgadhi on his language, which was different from the former. Even though Pāli was popularly called as Māgadhi, due to several reasons it is a composite language, which is an admixture of different regional dialects. In other words, despite being the language of Magadha Pāli remains distinct from Māgadhi Prākr̥t.

In this connection Geiger refers to an event from *Culla-vagga* of the Pāli *Vinayapiṭaka* according to which when two brāhmaṇa bhikkhus reported to the Buddha that people of different castes and creeds were polluting Buddha's teaching by keeping it in their diverse tongues and hence they would keep Buddha Vacana in "Chandas" (*handamayam bhante*

16. *Ibid.*, p. 17.

budhavaçanam chandaso āropamati) Budhaghoṣa interprets the word "Chandaso" as below:

> *chandaso āropemāti vedam viya sakkatabhāṣāya vācanamaggam āropema.*

Here the word "Chandas" indicates only ancient Āryan language in which Vedic Saṁhitās were written. Hence Buddhaghoṣa interprets the word "Chandaso" as that respected language, which is on par with Veda. In response to their proposal, the Buddha while saying it would be sinful act, categorically said:

> *anujānāmi bhikkave sakkāyaniruttiyā buddha vacanam pariyā punātu*

According to the grammatical rules of syntactical interpretation, prevalent during Buddhaghoṣa's times it is rendered in English as follows:

> "Bhikkhus, I permit you to learn Buddha-Vacanna
> in the language of the Buddha, i.e., "Māgadhi."
>
> *ettha sakānirutti nāma sammā sambuddhena vuttappakāro māgadhako voharo.*

Stages in the Development of the Pāli Language

A close study of Pāli literature reveals that there are four stages of development of Pāli language, which are given below:

(i) The Pāli language of Gāthā portions of *Tripiṭaka*,

(ii) The Pāli language of prose portions of the Pāli *Tripiṭaka*,

(iii) The Pāli language of later prose literature

(iv) The Pāli language of later Pāli Kāvyas.

Of the above, the language of the Gāthā portions in Pāli *Tripiṭaka* is the oldest, being the regional language of mid-India of Buddha's time and also of early Vedic Saṁhitās. It consists of many forms of Vedic language. The Language of *Sutta-Nipāta* is the best example of this type of language. There is greater uniformity in the second, viz. the Pāli language of prose portions of the *Tripiṭaka* as compared to the language of Gāthā portions. The development of new forms is the main characteristic of this type. The language of Pāli *Jātaka* is the example of this type. The prose language of *Tripiṭaka* is the basis of the language of the third stage. The language of the *Milindapañha* and Buddhaghoṣa's *Aṭṭahakathās* are the best examples of this type. Here we find a more evolved and noble style. Lastly the later Pāli Kāvyas are written in the style of literature of olden times. The growing impact of Sanskrit is the chief characteristic of this literature. The language of this fourth stage may be illustrated by the Vaṁsa literature of Ceylonese Chronicles, viz. the *Mahāvaṁsa*, the *Dīpavaṁsa*, the *Dhātavaṁsa* and the *Telekatāha gāthā*, a Pāli Sataka written about 12 *c.* CE.

Contribution of Scholars and Institutions to Pāli Language and Literature

Far Eastern Japanese scholars like Takakusu, Anesaki, D.T. Suzuki, Watanabe, H. Nakamura, Ceylonese scholars like G.P. Malalasekera, Anagarika Dharmapāla and P.N. Perera, Goonaratna, K.S. Jayatilleke, W.A. De Silva and Ven. Narada Mahathera, Burmese scholars like Shwe Zan Aung, Levi Sadaw, P. Maung Tin and Indian luminaries like Dhammananda Kosambi, B.M. Barua, B.C. Law, Satischandra Vidyabhusana, Saratchandra Das and P.V. Bapat contributed on different aspects of Pāli language by their numerous expositions, translations and learned research papers. In the West scholars like Trenckner, R.C. Childers, Anderson, Turnour, Fausboll, Pischel, T.W. Rhys Davids and C.A.F. Rhys Davids, A.B. Keith, W. Geiger. Robert Chalmers, E.J. Thomas, La Vallee Poussin, M. Winternitz, Mabel Bode, Stede, F.L. Woodward, to mention only a few have rendered immense service to the cause of study of Pāli by way of editing and translating many original Pāli texts and publishing monographs on Pāli language and literature.

The Pāli Text Society, London has done yeoman service by not only publishing the entire Pāli *Tripiṭaka* in Roman character but also by bringing out its English translations. In Ceylon, Burma and Thailand various editions of Pāli *Tripiṭaka* have been published since 1958. The Buddhist Publication Society in Kandy, Sri Lanka has been publishing English translations of Buddhist texts and a large number of expositions on Theravāda Buddhism through its Wheel series and Bodhi leaves. Since 1961, the Ministry of Cultural Affairs, The Government of Sri Lanka has been publishing "*Encyclopaedia of Buddhism*" in a series of volumes.

In Indian States of West Bengal and Bihar, Pāli was offered at Graduate and Post Graduate levels. In the University of Calcutta, Banaras Hindu University, Sampurnanda Sanskrit University, Varanasi, Magadh and Delhi Universities the Pāli Language and Literature have been studied at Post Graduate level.

Significance of the Study of Pāli Language

From various points of view the study of Pāli bears great significance.

(a) The study of Pāli, which is foremost and important among the Āryan languages of medieval times, has been neglected. The high antiquity of Pāli, its refinement, its verbal and grammatical simplicity, and its relationship with the oldest Vedic language testifies its unique character. In order to understand the present form of our languages the study of Pāli in a scientific way is essential.

(b) Pāli Language has not only influenced modern Indian languages such as Bengali, Oriya, Assamese, Hindi, Marathi, and Maithili, etc., but also had sufficient impact on the languages of Burma, Siam, Cambodia, Laos and other Buddhist countries which contain ample materials traceable directly or indirectly to Pāli.

(c) Even from the point of view of its literature the study of Pāli has great significance. Lord Buddha's teachings consist moral idealism, its object being an effort to show to mankind how to attain the goal of perfect human ideal. The contents of *Tripiṭaka* and its beautiful style stand parallel to any other literature. If mankind aspires liberation from the phenomenal world, the Buddha's message should be widely propagated. The Pāli Literature also inspires to produce a literature. For example Pāli literature inspired many thinkers and writers of Hindi literature. In the vast literature of Pāli *Tripiṭaka* and commentaries, the creative elements which are untouched can be utilised for the benefit of society.

d) The study of Pāli is not merely important but an imperative that enables us to grasp the Indian history and linguistics. The valuation of the cultural treasure of this literature is not made so far. In order to decide the chronology of Indian history, Pāli literature plays a vital role among others. For instance the *Tripiṭaka* and *Anupiṭaka* literature is full of invaluable material of ancient Indian history. Further, by means of study of Pāli literature one can gain more insight into Indian geography. That is why stressing on the important contribution of Pāli, B.M. Barua remarks that Pāli has produced an extensive literature,

> Which is full of historical information, vivid in the description of things, technical in the employment of words and phrases, lively in human interests, inspiring in tone and dignified in expression.[17]

(e) From the perspective of religion and philosophy also the study of Pāli has great significance. Lord Buddha delivered his message through the medium of Pāli, which is the popular language with a view that the spirit of the *dhamma* could enrich all.[18] The Buddhist religion and philosophy, which has been introduced through Sanskrit texts has partial outlook. The actual personality of the Buddha and his original teachings may be grasped only in the light of Pāli literature. Further the greatest significance of Pāli literature lies in its inspiring the faithful to do spiritual practice.

(f) Pāli Literature is not merely the literature of one religious tradition or that of Theravāda Buddhism, but is the literature of universal mankind devoid of caste, creed, etc., if there is any universal nature among Indian languages; it is certainly in Pāli Language. It is called as "universal religion" since it is free from all superstitions, sacrificialism and ideal of God-head which create barriers among human beings.

(g) Pāli Language and its literature contribute to global peace through the medium of Buddha's teachings. By its study it is possible to strengthen our cultural ties and political relations with other nations.

Hence, while throwing light on its significant role D.L. Barua rightly observes:

---

17. B.M. Barua, *Ceylon Lectures.*, p. 133.
18. Acharya Buddharakshita, *op. cit.*, see. Introduction.

Pāli appears to have been in use in India and outside for many centuries as a distinct literary language, capable of expressing all shades of experience, forms of thought and interests of life.[19]

19. D.L. Barua, *op. cit.*, preface, p. v.

3

The Tripiṭaka Literature

Vinaya Piṭaka

The word *piṭaka* primarily meant "a basket containing manuscripts" and secondarily "traditionally handing on." The Pāli canonical literature consists of three such Piṭakas. Of these, the *Vinaya* provides an account of the Buddhist Order. It is broadly divided into (i) *Suttavibaṅga,* (ii) *Khaṇḍakas*, (iii) *Parivāra,* (iv) *Pāṭimokkha.* This Piṭaka deals with the rules and regulations[1] of the administration of Buddhist Saṅgha; rules for the daily life of monks and nuns, admission into the Buddhist Saṅgha, rules pertaining to food, housing, clothing, medical treatment, periodical confession of sins, etc. laid down by the Buddha for their promulgation in order to establish morality (*śīla*) the very foundation stone on which the entire edifice of Buddhist Saṅgha has been established.

Sutta Piṭaka

The *Sutta Piṭaka* is the collection of doctrinal expositions both large and small. The Suttas are usually in prose occasionally interpreted with verses. They are the most important literary part of the Buddhist literature. The *Sutta Piṭaka* means the

---

1. S. Dutt, Early *Buddhist Monachism*, pp. 72-73, I.B. Horner, *the Book of Discipline*, I, p. xii, Charles S. Prebish, *Vinaya and Pratimoksha,* The Foundation of Buddhist Ethics in K. Narain (ed.) *Studies in History of Buddhism*, p. 223 ff.

basket of the *suttas* (Sanskrit "*sūtra*"), which means short "aphorisms." The term is used in a new sense of a doctrine "text" or a "lecture." Every explanation, very often in the form of a dialogue of one or more points of religion is called a Sutta. The *Sutta Piṭaka* contains five such Nikāyas or collections of Suttas. For an understanding of Buddhist religion the *Sutta Piṭaka* is most important as it is the best and most reliable source for the religion of the Buddha and his earliest disciples. It is the basket of discourses delivered by the Buddha during his forty-five years of active ministry. As regards the compilation of the Nikāyas, which belong to the *Sutta Piṭaka*, it is said that they are compiled soon after the Parinirvāṇa of the Buddha. They are presumed to have been recited during first Buddhist council held at Rājagr̥ha. There is a great probability of contending that all the five Nikāyas of the *Sutta Piṭaka* must have been in existence as early as third century BC at the earliest and first century CE at the latest. An intensive study of some early Barhut inscriptions reveal that as early as second century BC a Buddhist canon in the form of *Tripiṭaka*, which was divided into five Nikāyas, was in existence.[2] Whereas the *Vinaya Piṭaka* is the best source of information for the ancient Buddhist order, the life of the monks and the nuns in Buddhist Saṅgha, the *Sutta Piṭaka* is the reliable source of the Dharma of the Buddha's ethical teachings. The *Sutta Piṭaka* contains prose dialogues and legends. It is classified into five Nikāyas, namely the *Dīgha Nikāya*, the *Majjhima Nikāya*, the *Saṁyutta Nikāya*, the *Aṅguttara Nikāya*, and the *Khuddaka Nikāya*.

Of the above, the *Dīgha Nikāya* consists of thirty-four long Suttas. Every Sutta of the long dialogues of the *Dīgha Nikāya* is independent and discusses one or several points of the

2. Dipak Kumar Barua, *An Analytical Study of Four Nikāyas*, p. 6.

Buddhist doctrine. It is divided into three parts namely Śīlakkhandha Vagga, Mahāvagga and Paṭika Vagga.[3] Some of the important Suttas of this Nikāya are the *Brahmajāla Sutta,* the *Tevijja,* and the *Mahānidāna.* The *Mahāparinibbāna Sutta* is the most important Sutta, which furnishes us information about the last period of the Buddha's life and his last utterances before death. This Sutta also provides some information on the biography of the Buddha and is considered as the most ancient and authentic part of the Pāli canon.

The *Majjhima Nikāya,* the second book of the *Sutta Piṭaka,* which consists of one hundred and fifty two Suttas, contains dialogues and discourses of medium length[4] on manifold subjects. Some of the important Suttas of this collection are the *Mūlapariyāya,* the *Vatthupama,* the *Cūla-Māluṅkya,* the *Tevijja-Vacchagotta,* and the *Brahmāyu.* We come across discourses on all points of religion such as the four Noble Truths, the doctrine of *karma,* refutation of the soul theories, the goal of *Nirvāṇa,* different modes of meditation and so on. This Nikāya provides us a thorough picture of ancient Indian Life. This collection of the Middle length sayings also throws light on such themes as the Life of Buddhist monks, Brāhmaṇa sacrifices, forms of asceticism, the Buddha's interaction with Jains and the social and political conditions prevailing during his times.

In the *Saṁyutta Nikāya,* the third collection of the *Sutta Piṭaka,* there are five groups of *suttas,* viz. *Sagātha, Nidāna, Khandha, Saḷāyatana* and *Mahāvaggas* — which treat a definite topic or subject. This collection deals with the legends of fairies, gods and devils, with royal and priestly interviewers of Buddha. This book of kindred sayings lays emphasis on the Buddha's teachings concerning psycho-ethical and

3. *Ibid.,* p. 403.
4. *Ibid.,* p. 460.

philosophical themes.[5] The most important of the collection is the *Dhamma Chakka Pavattana Sutta* which contains the first sermon delivered by the Buddha when he commenced his mission as a religious teacher.

In the *Aṅguttara Nikāya,* the fourth collection of the *Sutta Piṭaka,* Suttas are arranged according to numerical succession. This Piṭaka is divided into eleven Nipātas divided into chapters that vary from 3 to 26, which consists of 2,308 *suttas.*[6] A number of *sutta*s of this collection shed light on the development of Buddhism and its history. All the *sutta*s lay special emphasis on the two-fold *Vinaya,* viz. the *Bhikku* and *Gahapati Vinaya*s.[7] First comes the things whose number is one, then whose number is two, and three and so on. For example, "two bright things," "two sorts of Buddhas," etc. The "three division" relates to triad of deeds, words and thoughts, three sorts of monks, three god-messengers, etc. On account of this scholastic grouping of material the *Aṅguttara Nikāya* comes nearer to the *Abhidamma Piṭaka.*

The *Khuddaka Nikāya* is the collection of minor anthologies and is the fifth and the last division of the *Sutta Piṭaka.* It is the largest of the five divisions of the *Sutta Piṭaka.* Most of these works are composed in verse. The *Khuddaka Nikāya* is a treasure of Buddhist poetry. It is composed of fifteen short miscellaneous treatises. The whole set of these fifteen independent treatises is also called "*Khuddakagantha.*"

The *Khuddaka Nikāya* is so named after the title of the first text of the collection, viz. *Khuddakapāṭha.*[8] The title of this

5. *Ibid.*, p. 540.
6. *Ibid.*, p. 575, B.C. Law, *A History of Pāli Literature,* vol. I, p. 180.
7. B.C. Law, *op. cit.*, p. 191.
8. R.B. Adhikari, "Khuddaka-Nikāya" in *Encyclopaedia of Buddhism,* vol. VI, Fascile 2, p. 207.

collection, viz. *Khuddaka Nikāya* is justified firstly because, as viewed by Oliver Abeynayake,[9] the collection of the texts are traditionally considered as less important since they are composed by the disciples or by the Buddha's followers as compared with the first four Nikāyas which contain the discourses preached directly by the Buddha himself, and secondly, as Warder asserts,[10] due to their doubtful authenticity as collected texts in the Minor Tradition.

These fifteen works are independent and belong to different times both very early and earliest as well as the latest stratums of the Pāli canon. The *Khuddaka Nikāya* not only combines books of different periods but also probably of different schools as well. Thus the *Khuddaka Nikāya* is the collection of heterogeneous elements in contrast to the homogeneous nature of the four Nikāyas.

The *Khuddaka Nikāya* seems to have developed sometime during the Buddha's lifetime and the date of the third Buddhist council.[11] Rhys Davids draws our attention to the inscriptional evidence of 3 *c.* BC which testifies the existence of the five Nikāyas through the term "*Pañca-Nekāyika.*" From this we may infer with much certainty that by the time of Buddhaghoṣa's visit to Sri Lanka in 5 *c.* AD the *Khuddaka Nikāya* was in existence in its complete form.[12] The *Milindapañha* of 1 *c.* AD. also refers to the knowledge of the bhikkus of those times in the five Nikāyas.[13]

---

9. O. Abeynayake, *A Textual and Historical Analysis of the Khuddaka Nikāya,* p. 16.
10. A.K. Warder, *Indian Buddhism,* pp. 202-03.
11. Ruwan Bandara Adhikari, "Khuddaka-Nikāya" *Encyclopaedia of Buddhism,* vol. VI, Fasc. 2, p. 208.
12. *Ibid.*, p. 209.
13. *Ibid.*, p. 208.

We come across either references to *Khuddaka Nikāya* or about some works of its collection in the Pāli Commentarial literature. For instance, according to Buddhaghoṣa's *Vinaya Aṭṭhakathā*, the *Khuddaka Nikāya* consists of all sayings of the Buddha which are not contained in the other four Nikāyas. Despite not referring to a collection called *Khuddaka Nikāya* the *Sumaṅgala Vilāsinī* mentions that eleven treatises included in the *Abhidhāmma Piṭaka* which belongs to the present collection of the *Khuddaka Nikāya* were rehearsed by the Dīghabhānakas to which three more were added by the *Majjhimabhānakas* who included them under the *Suttapiṭaka*.

The fifteen books, which belong to the collection of *Khuddha Nikāya* are *Khuddha Pāṭha* or short passages; *Dhammapada* or the collection of moral precepts, *Udāna* or short lyrics; *Itivuttaka* or sayings of the Buddha; *Sutta Nipāta* or didactic poems, *Vimānavattu* or stories of celestial mansions, *Petavattu* or treatise on the departed spirits, *Theragāthā* or the *gāthās* composed by the monks, *Therigāthā* or the *gāthās* composed by the nuns, *Jātakas* or stories of the Buddha's former births, *Niddesa* or a treatise on the explanation on the *Sutta Nipāta, Paṭisambhidāmagga* or a treatise on Arhat's analytical knowledge, *Apadāna* or a treatise on the legends about Arhants or Saints, *Buddhavaṁsa* or a work on the lives of preceding Buddha and Gautama Buddha and the *Cariyāpiṭaka* or a treatise on Gautama's deeds in former births collected in versified form. According to the Burmese tradition four other works namely, the *Milinda Pañha*, the *Sutta Saṅgaha*, the *Kuddakapāṭha* and the *Nettippakarana* are also included in the collection of the *Khuddaka Nikāya*.

In the view of M. Winternitz, a historian,[14] the *Khuddaka Nikāya* is the collection of smaller pieces. But according to

---

14. M. Winternitz, *A History of Indian Literature*, vol. II. P. 76.

scholars like R.S. Adhikari,[15] none of the English renderings of the term "*Khuddaka*," viz. "small, mean, less important, younger and inferior" seem appropriate in view of the nature of the *Khuddaka* texts some of which are large anthologies and some works are significant literary compositions and some others enunciate the present Buddhist philosophical teachings. The composition of the *Khuddaka Nikāya* indicates some significant passages found in the *Saṁyutta Nikāya* and *Aṅguttara Nikāya*. The contents of the collection of the *Khuddaka Nikāya* include aphorisms, songs, poems, fairy tales and fables. According to the commentary on the *Khuddakapāṭha* known as the *Paramatthajotikā*,[16] *Khuddaka Nikāya* is a miscellaneous collection of short and variegated *dhamma*. The unstable character of the *Khuddaka Nikāya* is evident from the inclusion of the four texts mentioned above by the Burmese Buddhists and the exclusion of the eight texts from the Siamese edition of the Pāli canon. Moreover the *Khuddaka Nikāya* does not appear as a whole in the Chinese Āgamas. Some of the contents of the books found in the *Khuddaka Nikāya* are seen common in other literary works.

Abhidhamma Piṭaka

The third division of the *Tripiṭaka* is the *Abhidhamma Piṭaka* known as "Basket of higher expositions" or "Transcendental Doctrine." As distinguished from the Sutta, the *Abhidhamma* is regarded as the "Higher Doctrine" with reference to the arrangement and treatment of its contents. Modern scholars like Venerable U. Revata and Bhikkhu Bodhi assert[17] that the *Abhidhamma Piṭaka* is the heart of *Abhidhamma* philosophy.

---

15. R.B. Adhikari, *op. cit.*, p. 207.
16. *Ibid.*, p. 208.
17. Ven. Bhikkhu Bodhi (Rev. tr.) Ven. Narada *Mahāthera's A Comprehensive Manual of Abhidhamma*, See Introduction, p. 1.

Similar to the *Sarvāstivādin Abhidhamma Piṭaka,* which is extant in the Chinese version, the *Pāli Abhidhamma Piṭaka* of the *Theravāda* school consists of seven books, viz. (i) *Dhamma-Saṅganī,* (ii) *Vibhaṅga,* (iii) *Dhātu-Kathā,* (iv) *Puggla-paññatti,* (v) *Kathāvatthu,* (vi) *Yamaka,* and (vii) *Paṭṭhāna.*

Based on the internal evidence of this collection, scholars like Cassius A. Pereira opine[18] that among the seven books listed above the *Dhamma Saṅganī,* the *Vibhaṅga* and the *Paṭṭhāna* are the oldest and they were recited at the second Buddhist Council held in 4 *c.* BC. These were followed by the Dhātu-Katha, the Puggla-Paññatti and the Yamaka which are pre-Aśokan and were recited during the third Buddhist Council. During the third Buddhist Council at Paṭaliputra the details of the *Kathāvattu* were outlined. The whole *Abhidhamma-Piṭaka* is believed to have been in existence before 250 BC.

In *Theravāda* perspective, there does not exist in the absolute sense (Paramaṭṭha) any real, self-dependent, permanent "entity" or "ego" except ever-changing process of conditionally arising and passing phenomena. The sole objective of the entire *Abhidhamma Piṭaka* is merely "to describe, analyse and elucidate"[19] such transient phenomena. That is why scholars like Nayanatiloka affirm[20] that the *Abhidhamma-Piṭaka* attempts to systematise and elucidate the doctrines of the *Sutta Piṭaka* from the psychological and physiological rather than philosophical standpoint.

---

18. Nyanatiloka Mahāthera, *Guide Through the Abhidhamma — Piṭaka,* See. C.A. Pereira's Foreward, p. xi.
19. *Ibid.,* Introduction, p. 3.
20. *Ibid.,* Introduction, p. 1.

4

Theravāda and Mahāyāna Buddhism

THERAVĀDA BUDDHISM

Salient Features of Theravāda

The whole teaching of the Buddha can be summed up in the word *dhamma*, the law of righteousness. The Buddha appealed to mankind to lead a noble, charitable and compassionate life. The *dharma* preached by the Buddha helps us from the world of sorrow and suffering to the blissful state of *nirvāṇa*, which is the highest goal of every spiritual aspirant. There is no external saviour or redeemer in the Buddha's doctrine. Only through one's self-effort and transformation of one's own character, an individual attains *nirvāṇa* the summum bonum of life. There is no recourse to God, scripture, etc. in the traditional sense of the term in Buddhism.

The Buddha emphatically denied the dogmatic opinions and fanciful speculations. His objective is to search the truth. He never entertained the idea of the first cause. He advocated always to do good, to avoid evil and purify one's mind. His approach is rational, self-introspection. In order to accomplish the goal of *nirvāṇa* one should also have devotion along with reasoned knowledge. Whereas reason enables human being to arrange the systematic knowledge, devotion provides determination to pursue the ideal of life. Thus reason and devotion hand-in-hand will enable an aspirant to realize the truth. There is three-fold refuge in Buddhism namely: taking refuge in the Buddha, in the *dharma* and Saṅgha. The ideal of the Buddha as personification of the enlightenment gives us inspiration to fight out the evil in the existence until it is totally overcome. By taking refuge in the *dharma* one can truly express gratitude for the Buddha since it is the only path for the annihilation of the suffering. The Buddhist Saṅgha, which consists of those ideal and sincere followers of laymen, laywomen, monks and nuns preserves the *dharma* and unique spirit of the noble teaching. Its role is to propagate the *dharma* and hand it over to the next generation. Ignorance only creates sin, which begets suffering. This dynamics of existence is a cyclic process, which goes on from eternity to eternity (ad infinitum).

Doctrine of Dependent Origination

The Buddha put forward the doctrine of dependent origination (*paṭiccasamuppāda*) according to which even though elements (*dhamma*) are not connected with each other by any pervading stuff in space-time continuum their manifestation is governed by the laws of causation (*hetu-paccaya*) and the evanescent elements are not subject to a haphazard process (*adicca-samuppanna*). Although, every element appears only for a single moment it is in fact "dependently originating element." Since the origin of every element depends on a preceding element or elements, existence is defined as "dependent existence" (*paṭiccasamuppāda*) expressed by the canonical formula:

> If there is this, there come to be that (*asmim sati, idam bhāvati*)[1]

The Buddha illustrated this by the example of the wheel of existence (*bhāva chakra*). According to the Buddha, it is not

---

1. C.A. Moore, *The Indian Mind*, p. 78.

wise to think or speculate whether the world is eternal or not. The phenomenal existence is conditioned by certain causes. The dependent origination enunciates that there is a wheel of life consists of "twelve" links or steps of cause and effect. These are ignorance (*avijjā*), conformation (*saṅkhāra*), consciousness (*viññāṇa*), name and form (*nāmarūpa*), six organs (*saḍāyatana*), contact (*phassa*), sensation (*vedanā*), desire (*taṇhā*) attachment (*upādāna*), formation of being (*bhāva*), birth (*jāti*), and old age and death (*jarā Maraṇa*). Of the twelve links ignorance and craving are the keynote of the wheel of existence. Ignorance is the main cause of the present existence. Ignorance is the nerve center of the existential flame. It produces blind activity. It gives rise to conformations. This is a stage of both the preparation and to prepare. It is a process of self-generation. The saṅkhāra gives rise to consciousness. It is the germ of the new being. From consciousness arise the name and form (*nāmarūpa*). This is the stage of prenatal growth where the mind and body are combined. Without consciousness name and form would not arise. In the words of the Buddha name and form constitute the (individual) human being. The name and form further leads to the stage of six organs of sense (*saḍāyatana*). These include our "five" sense organs and the mind. The six organs of sense produce "contact" (*phassa*). Through the "six" sense-organs the individual's state of activity begins in the world. From the six sense organs spring perception or sensation (*vedanā*). Here the individuality of the living being is recognized. From this stage onwards the individual enters the true sphere of self-creation. Perception gives rise to desire and the individual begins to develop varied experiences such as pleasure, pain and neutral feeling. Desire produces attachment. It means to make one's own feeling whether pleasant, unpleasant or neutral. This attachment (*upādāna*) is the effort to retain the object of desire. The grasping of a thing leads to the formation of being (*bhāva*). It means the tendency "to be." The individual spins his future from the present and his present is conditioned by the past. The formation of being further leads the individual to birth (*jāti*). From birth old age, disease and death necessarily follows. When one's physical form is disintegrated the conformations which are "micro-psychic-corpuscles" transmigrate into the next existence. So long as one's desire lasts the series of rebirth recur again and again. According to the Buddha, without the knowledge of the dependent origination one cannot progress towards the goal of *nirvāṇa*. A true Buddhist should never repent for the past. For a spiritual aspirant present is more crucial which is in his hands. Everything depends on motivation. The present is born due to the past. In the present we are in the grip of law of existence. In the present existence we ignorantly spin our future. Just as a potter shapes the pot one can mould one's future by moulding the present.

Doctrine of Non-self (Anattā)

The fundamental characteristics of all existence from Buddhist perspective are suffering (*dukkha*) impermanence (*aniccā*) and substancelessness (*anattā*). There are "five" aggregates (*khaṇḍa*) known as corporeality, feeling, perception, mental formations and consciousness. Neither the objective world nor the subjective self are static. In mental sphere "Mind is not an entity but a function."[2] The Buddha denied a unifying principle such as soul. The soul or self is just a name given to the collective actions put together of mind and body. According to the *Milindapañha* of the *Khuddaka Nikāya*, in the dialogue between Bhikshu Nāgasena and King Milinda the former clarifies all the doubts about the nature of the self. According to this text "soul" is a name just like a "chariot" is a name to the sum total

2. *Ibid.*, p. 76.

of its constituent parts. Just as the "chariot" is not equal to any one of its parts singly, similarly "soul" is not equal to any one of the five consciousnesses. The consciousness is a stream of moments.

The phenomenal existence is impermanent since the beings are transformed in uninterrupted psychophysical activity from one life to another. It is non-self and unsubstantial since it is a ceaseless becoming and eternal cyclic operation endlessly changing from one existence to another. As it is always in the process of continuous change it is full of suffering. *Nirvāṇa* is the state, which is free from the flux of the existence.

Doctrine of Karma and Rebirth

According to Lord Buddha, the word *kamma* refers to all kinds of volitional acts of both moral and immoral nature. In Buddhism the present is real and it demands realization to appropriate one's own action for the attainment of the goal of *nirvāṇa*. *Karma* is the universal law of cause and effect. According to the Buddha, *kamma* is not a fatalistic entity which goes from one life to another. Life is the product of *kamma*.[3] Thought, speech and action reap results depending upon one's intention. The Buddha didn't entertain and also encourage the speculation about the ultimate aspect of *karma* and its first beginnings. This is regarded as futile debate to discuss metaphysical questions, which have no relevance in human situation. *Karma* operates in the broad stream of life. A human being is solely responsible for both happiness and suffering in this world. The novelty in human existence is that a conscious being has certain amount of free will, which enables the individual to mould one's life and modify actions. In Buddhist way of life there is more emphasis on the knowledge of *karma*. One who understands the true nature of *karma* begets patience,

3. See. G.P. Malalasekera, *Some Aspects of reality as taught by Theravāda Buddhism* in C.A. Moore, *op. cit.*, p. 79.

which further keeps him confident and discernible. Self-restraint, self-reliance and self-confidence are the true cardinal virtues of a human being who is conversant with the knowledge of *karma* and dependent origination. The practice of good *karma* in course of time will free the individual from the wheel of the suffering and keeps an aspirant on the track of the goal of life, i.e., *nirvāṇa*.

The principle of dependent origination and the law of *karma* provide the background for understanding the nature of rebirth. Death is not the end of the human being. When only one's physical form is annihilated the conformations transmigrate into the next existences. One's physical form is only an outward manifestation of the invisible karmic force, which takes one form or the other due to the effects of the intentions as well as actions in one's past life. The stream of consciousness is compared with the flow of running water. Due to the law of dependent origination transmigration of consciousness takes place as rebirth. Just as the vibrations of the musical note cease when the tuning fork to the particular note stops, similarly when the karmic effects are no longer latent in human being they render the rebirth without locus. In the Milinda-Nāgasena dialogue referred to above the continuity of existence of a person or a thing is explained as follows: Although the light comes from the same lamp the flames in different periods of night are not the same, yet they look identical. According to Nāgasena, the oneness of the personality of personal identity is understood by the illustrations such as milk and curd, butter and *ghee* although the manifestations arise from the same milk. A true Buddhist is aware that one's present is more crucial and therefore it motivates him to make use of the present, and to mould the future by leading a righteous life. Meditation and concentration equip human being with a power to look at the mechanics of causality with diligence. According to Buddhist stand point, we come out of the past actions of virtues and vices. The present is born due to the past. We go to the effects of causation. Here Buddhism in opposition to the eternal cycle of suffering offers to us the solution. Practice of Buddhist ideals, knowledge of dependent origination, belief in the nature of *karma*, and cultivation of universal love leads the spiritual aspirant towards perfection and insight.

Doctrine of Four Noble Truths

To end influx of *karma* insight into the four noble truths is the only remedy. Whatever may be the form of the existence, the four are invariably present in them. They are: the noble truths of suffering, the origin of suffering, the extinction of suffering and the path that leads to the extinction of suffering. Whoever develops the insight into the above four noble truths is said to have the right knowledge. The knowledge of four noble truths dispels the ignorance, which perpetuates desire and delusion. Of the above, the first noble truth is summarized as below: birth is suffering, decay is suffering, death is suffering, willing is suffering, having something is suffering, losing is suffering. Thus, the phenomenal existence is constituted with various facets of suffering. The origin of suffering is due to craving for experience. Craving involves an incessant effort to get an object for new experience. This consciousness of new experience in turn becomes the cause of another experience and thus the process of craving multiplies eternally. Thus, the Buddhist sees the world as a state of continuous suffering. This is not to be wrongly understood as mere pessimism and feeling of melancholy, since for everybody who leads righteous life there is possibility of deliverance from suffering. The chief source of suffering is ignorantly identifying mind-body with "I" or "mine." The origin of suffering is due to craving for experience. In answer to the question what is responsible for the thirst of the being: which leads from one birth to another, the doctrine of dependent origination was enunciated. The truth concerning the extinction of suffering reveals that there is a way, which can completely deliver us from suffering. Among the twelve links of the chain of the dependent origination, ignorance and craving are the important links to be dissolved. The ideal of the noble eight-fold path is the programme which establishes one leading to the goal of complete extinction of suffering.

Doctrine of Noble Eight-Fold Path

The noble eight-fold path is the way which comprises eight steps, namely: right understanding, right thought, right speech, right action, right livelihood, right effort, right mindfulness and right concentration. This is known as the middle path (*majjhima paṭipada*), which keeps away a person from two extremes known as self-indulgence and self-mortification.[4] This reminds us of the golden means suggested by Aristotle in post-Socratic period.

Of the above, right view (*sammā-diṭṭhi*) means the understanding of the four noble truths given above. The second limb, viz. "right thought" is also known as right resolve or right aspiration (*sammā-saṅkappa*) is a faculty to discern the good from the bad and frees a person from lust, ill will and cruelty. The third limb right-speech (*sammā-vācā*) means talking only auspicious things and abstaining from lies, tale-bearing harsh language and unworthy conversation. The fourth is right action (*sammā-kammanta*), which means abstaining from killing, stealing and illegal sexual relations. Right livelihood (*sammā-ājīva*) is a living by just means. It means non-injurious and non-harmful living. Right effort or right exertion (*sammā-*

4. *Ibid.*, pp. 68-69.

vāyāma) is a mature action in human relationship. It means that one should have confidence and restraint in actions. Right-mindfulness (*sammā-sati*) is a contemplation on the four fundamentals of mindfulness namely contemplation of the body, feeling, mind and mind-objects. Vigilant attention leads one to see things in the right perspective. One must be conscious of environment and actions. Perfect attention is a means to obtain right knowledge to understand reality. Right-concentration (*sammā-samādhi*) is the concentration on a simple object, which is associated with wholesome consciousness. The practice and cultivation of mindfulness results in the development of concentration. Refraining from all evil-doing, doing what is good and purifying one's mind are the three stages of the development which are designed to dispel defilements. The practice of right concentration helps an aspirant to live justly and to understand things rightly. An aspirant must win the goal of purity only through one's self-effort. Neither the Buddha nor the gods can deliver mankind from suffering by their efforts.

The practice of moral life is the very core and essence of Buddhism. Morality makes a man gentle in his speech and concentration controls the mind and makes him calm, serene and steady. Finally wisdom enables a spiritual aspirant to overcome all the defilements completely. There are three stages by which one proceeds to the goal of *arhant*, viz. the path-enterer; the once-returner and non-returner. Any spiritual aspirant who enters the Buddhist order and aims at the goal of *arhant* has to attain these three preliminary stages. One reaches the stage of *arhant* when he begins to realize that there is no self or a single principle underlying the reality of existence. He sees that all things are conditioned, impermanent and subject to suffering. The *arhant* is free from lust, hatred and delusion. *Nirvāṇa* is the freedom when one's desire is completely extinguished. It is total emancipation from one's ignorance.[5]

MAHĀYĀNA BUDDHISM

Emergence of Mahāyāna, its Home and Antiquity

According to Mahāyāna Buddhist tradition Mahāyāna originated from the Buddha's teaching delivered to the large assembly of Bodhisattvas on the mount of Vulture Peak (Gṛdhrakūṭa) in Rājagṛha known as the "Second Turning of the wheel of righteousness" (*dvitīya dharmachakra pravartana*). The internal textual evidence of two *Mahāyāna-Sūtras*, viz. the *Saddharma Puṇḍarīka* and the *Sandhinirmocana* respectively refer to the turning of the wheel of Law twice and thrice by the Buddha.[6] Various traditional interpretations from China, Japan and Tibet which divide the teaching schedule of the Buddha into five periods hold that the first, third, fourth and fifth periods consist of *Mahāyāna-Sūtras*[7]; of them during the first period, i.e., the few weeks after his enlightenment the *Avataṁsaka-Sūtra* was delivered.[8]

Attesting this traditional view, Bhikṣu Saṅgharakshita asserts[9] that the Mahāyānists always believe that the fundamental tenets of their school were actually taught by the Buddha. The *Mahāyāna-Sūtras* are the direct utterances of Śākyamuni, which were delivered in early and later phases of his life. According to another view based on the standpoint of Japanese scholars, although the Buddha cannot be regarded

---

5. *Ibid.*, pp. 81-82.
6. G.C. Pandy, *Studies in Mahāyāna*, p. 14.
7. *Ibid.*,
8. *Ibid.*, p. 13.
9. Bhikshu Sangharakshita, *A Survey of Buddhism*, p. 262.

as the author of the *Mahāyāna-Sūtras*, the distinctively Mahāyāna doctrines found in these works were first taught by him to his more advanced disciples who in turn transmitted them esoterically from generation to generation until the appropriate time to reveal them to the world. S.R. Goyal a noted writer on History of Indian Buddhism contends[10] that the Mahāyāna grew out of Theravāda, (i.e., Hīnayāna) though it traces its final authority to Buddha himself. The Theravādin conception of the Buddha as omniscient, endowed with supernormal powers, his pre-eminence over all beings including *arahants*, his identification with the *dhamma* on the one hand and *nibbāna* on the other, his characterization as numinous principle, transcendent, infinite and blessed (*bhagavā*); the Buddha's deification by Mahāsaṅghikas and their offshoots in course of time appears to have shaped the Mahāyāna Buddha ideal. As Saṅgharakshita rightly describes:

> The Mahāyāna is a movement not of innovation but of development and unfoldment.[11]

Har Dayal contends that the rise of Mahāyāna resulted not only from its latent tendencies traced in the early Buddhism but also due to the influence of Indian religious sects like the Bhāgavatas and Śaivas, Persian religion and culture, Greek art and Christianity, etc.[12] As regards the antiquity of Mahāyāna, during post-Theravāda period some time between 1 *c.* BC - 1 *c.* CE. Mahāyāna is believed to have emerged from the embryonic shell of the Mahāsaṅghika Buddhist sect. Nalinaksha Dutt thinks that the evolution of Mahāyāna took place in three stages of which the final stage marks the emergence of Mahāyāna during 1 *c.* CE when Prajñāpāramitā literature came into existence. N. Dutt and Poussin have argued

10. S.R. Goyal, *A History of Indian Buddhism*, p. 211.

11. Bhikshu Saṅgharakshita, *op. cit.*, p. 261.

12. *Ibid.*, p. 214.

that some time during the second half of 2 *c.* BC and 1 *c.* BC ideas similar to those of Mahāyāna appeared among Buddhist sects which served as the basis of *Mahāyāna-Sūtra*s. The works of Vasumitra and Nāgārjuna disclose the fact that *Mahāyāna-Sūtra*s were in existence as early as second half of 3 *c.* BC. In S.R. Goyal's view,[13] the traces of some of the Mahāyāna doctrines seemed to assume a definite shape at the close of first *c.* BC.

According to Masao Shizutani referred by Hajime Nakamura,[14] the incipient and developed stages of proto-Mahāyāna could be placed between 1 *c.* BC to 1 *c.* CE and the incipient and developed stages of early Mahāyāna could be fixed between 50 CE - 250 CE. G.C. Pande opines[15] that the beginnings of "ur-Mahāyānic literature" could go back to the semi-Mahāyānic sects of the 4th and 3 *c.* BC; the earliest extant *Mahāyāna-Sūtra*s arose between 100 BC - 200 CE. Some of these were enlarged and new Sūtras were added between 2 *c.* CE - 4*c.* CE. This is followed by the classics of *Mahāyāna-Sūtra* literature written between l *c.* CE - 7 *c.* CE by a galaxy of *ācārya*s namely Aśvaghoṣa, Nāgārjuna, Āryadeva, Maitreyanātha, Asaṅga, Vasubandhu, Diṅnāga and Dharmakīrti, Śāntideva, Śāntarakṣita and Kamalaśīla.

As regards the original home of Mahāyāna, based on the textual evidence of the *Aṣṭasāhasrikā Prajñāpāramitā* and *Ratnakūta-Sūtra*s, Goyal presumes[16] that Mahāyāna had its origins in Andhra of South India from where it spread to eastern regions, viz. Orissa, Bengal, and Bihar and then reached north-west by the age of Kaniṣka-1. G.C. Pandey affirms that the rise of Mahāyāna took place in Sātavāhana-

13. S.R. Goyal, *op. cit.*, p. 220.
14. H. Nakamura, *op. cit.*, p. 152.
15. G.C. Pande, *op. cit.*, p. 33.
16. S.R. Goyal, *op. cit.*, p. 222.

Kuṣāṇa age. Magadha, Orissa and Andhra were the early centres of Mahāyāna. It spread with Sātavāhanas westwards and northwards and reaching north-west flourished and expanded under the aegis of the Kuṣāṇas.

Meaning and Justification of the Term Mahāyāna

The term *yāna* or *yānam* rendered into English as "vehicle" is applied to both vehicles, i.e., Hīnayāna as well as Mahāyāna which are distinguished from one another. In a general sense *yāna* stands for a means to attain enlightenment and accordingly the term is suffixed to different schools of Buddhism, viz. Hīnayāna, Mahāyāna, Vajrayāna, Mantrayāna, Sahajayāna and Kālacakrayāna. In Mahāyāna philosophical context, the term *yāna* is also applied to vehicles, viz. Śrāvakayāna, Pratyeka Buddha-yāna and the Bodhisattva-yāna, which are different religious methods to attain spiritual goals.

At the second Buddhist council held at Vaiśālī (386-370 BC) the Theravādins excommunicated the Vajjian monks (who were later called as Mahāsaṅghikas) as holders of heretical doctrines (adhammavādins) and "sinful monks" (*pāpabhikṣus*). As a protest and in order to prove their superiority over Theravāda monks on the one hand and to brand them as inferior, the Mahāsaṅghikas were incited to coin the different terms such as Eka-yāna, Dviyāna, Śrāvaka-yāna, Bodhisattva-yāna, Buddha-yāna till they arrived at the invention of the terms Mahāyāna and Hīnayāna. While defining the four key terms of Mahāyāna tradition, the *Ratnaguṇa samuccaya gāthā* (which belongs to 1 *c.* BC) explains the term Bodhi-yāna differentiating it from the *arhant* ideal of Theravādins. The term "Mahāyāna" was coined after different synonymous terms used for Mahāyāna such as Eka-yāna, Bodhi-yāna, Buddha-yāna and Bodhisattva-Yana. The *Aṣṭasāhasrikā*

Prajñāpāramitā is probably the earliest work, which mentioned the term 'Mahāyāna.'

In the early *Mahāyāna-Sūtra* works such as the *Pañcavimsati-sāhasrikā Prajñāpāramitā*, the *Avataṁsaka* and the *Saddharma Puṇḍarīka,* which were in existence before Nāgārjuna, the term "Hīnayāna" and "Mahāyāna" are not used in a comparative sense. But these terms were later used in a comparative sense by a galaxy of *ācāryas*, viz. Aśvaghoṣa, Nāgārjuna, Āryadeva, Maitraya, Asaṅga, Vasubandhu, Sthiramati, Bhāvaviveka, Jñānaprabhā, Śāntideva, Dharmapāla and Śīlabhadra. Based on the philosophic and linguistic analysis, Buddhist *ācāryas* referred to above as well as Buddhalogists of modern times justified the term Mahāyāna by various interpretations. According to the *Aṣṭasāhasrikā* and *Daśasāhasrikā Prajñāpāramitā,* "Mahāyāna" is so-called because it is vast as the sky that leads both human and non-human beings. It is a receptacle for all sentient beings. Only Bodhisattvas can understand its beginning, middle and end, which are imperceptible to others. Owing to its equal dimensions on all sides "Mahāyāna" is called as "Great Vehicle."

Asaṅga states in his *Mahāyāna Sūtrālaṅkāra* that the Śrāvaka and Pratyeka Buddhayānists seek their own salvation as a consequence of which their path is known as *hīna*. As opposed to these, the Mahāyānists never seek their own salvation till others have attained it and consequently their path is "*mahā*" (superior). Further according to Asaṅga in Śrāvaka-yāna, the way of life for gathering merit and wisdom as well as the time taken for its practice and attainment of the above goal are all in a "small scale" in contrast to which in "Mahāyāna" all these are on a "large scale"; hence the Śrāvaka-yāna is "small" or "inferior" (*hīna*) and Mahāyāna is "great" or "superior" (*mahā*). While giving the philosophical explanation of the two *yānas*, the Mahāyāna works show that the Theravādins are taught only the means of the removal of the cover of impurities (*kleśāvaraṇa*), whereas the Mahāyānists are taught the means of the removal of the cover of impurities as well as the cover of ignorance (*jñeyāvaraṇa*). Hence owing to their superior attainment the Mahāyānists deserve the distinctive appellation *mahā*. For H. Nakamura[17] Mahāyāna is the great vehicle in a two-fold sense: Firstly it is a greater teaching than that of conservative Buddhism of Theravāda; secondly as it claims to deliver more people from suffering than Theravāda, Mahāyāna is superior to the former. G.C. Pandey remarks[18] that Mahāyāna is great or universal vehicle for all and ultimately the one or supreme vehicle "Ekayāna or Agrayāna" as it believed in the validity of alternative traditions for those with different dispositions. In Mahāyāna conception although the *dharma* is one and universal in essence, its historical manifestation took place in different ways depending on the diversity of human nature and character as well as their needs and capacities.

Salient Features of Mahāyāna Buddhism

According to early Mahāyāna works, the salient features of Mahāyāna are:

(i) The true nature of Tathāgata is ungraspable and inconceivable (*acintya*).

(ii) Buddha is conceived as Eternal Dharmakāya being identified with Absolute, first principle and essential cause of all existence (*dharmatā*).

(iii) All compounded things are Śūnya, which in their ultimate nature are non-dual and suchness (*tathatā*).

---

17. H. Nakamura, *op. cit.*, p.149.

18. G.C. Pande, *op. cit.*, p. 7.

(iv) Since all sentient beings potentially possess Buddha-hood, they will attain knowledge of Buddha-hood (*tathāgatajñāna*) sooner or later.

(v) The Mahāyānists evolved *Trikāya* conception of the Buddha, viz. the *Dharma-kāya*, the *Saṁbhoga-kāya* and the *Nirmāṇa-kāya*. Of these, the last two are the created forms and are the expedients devised by the skilful means of the *Dharma-kāya* Buddha who is identical with non-dual suchness (*tathatā*). The goal of a *Bodhi-sattva* is to realize the non-existence of the phenomenal world and thereby realize *Dharma-kāya*, which is the metaphysical principle of real *citta*, identical with *Tathatā, Dharmadhātu* and *Tathāgata-garbha*.

(vi) Recognition of innumerable Buddhas and Bodhisattvas who are compassionate saviours and redeemers of suffering humanity.

(vii) The altruistic principle of Bodhisattva's dedication of merit (*pariṇāmana*). The Bodhisattva ideal of Mahāyāna surpassed the Śrāvaka and Pratyeka Buddha ideals of early Buddhist schools. The Mahāyānic shift from *Arhant* to Bodhisattva ideal, its exclusive emphasis on Bodhisattva's compassion and universal altruism, the portrayal of Bodhisattvas who by dedication of merit (*pariṇāmana*) play the role of redeemers of suffering and saviours of humanity consequently led them to be regarded as the objects of faith and devotion.

(viii) The Mahāyāna Doctrine of salvation by faith and devotion to the Buddha and Bodhisattvas is the essential and only means to attain perfect enlightenment or Buddha-hood. Mahāyāna is highly emotional and devotional in attitude. The doctrine of salvation by faith and devotion comprises adoration and praise of the virtues of the Buddhas and Bodhisattvas, paying homage to them, invocation and recitation of their names and unflinching faith in their saving power. According to Santideva's *Bodhicaryāvatāra* the six constituents of supreme worship are (1) obeisance (*vandana*) and worship (*pūjā*) (2) going for refuge (*śaraṇa-gamana*). (3) confession of sins (*pāpa-desana*), (4) rejoicing in merit (*punyānumodana*), (5) Prayer (*adhyesana*), (6) Transfer of merit (*pariṇāmana*), and (7) self-surrender (*ātmabhāvādi-parityāgaḥ*).

(ix) Being progressive and liberal minded, Mahāyāna cares more for the spirit rather than the letter of the Buddha's utterances. Its conception of *nirvāṇa* is more positive. Mahāyāna positivism is of two kinds, viz. doctrinal and methodological. On the one hand from the doctrinal standpoint Mahāyāna maintained invalidity of all conjectural formulations of Reality both positive and negative. On the other hand from the methodological standpoint it recognized that positive formulation of Reality being more easily understood and more attractive than negative ones were of greater help to an average follower of Buddhism since they are efficacious as supports of the spiritual life. The Mahāyānists adopted this dual standpoint because on the one hand they want to safeguard the profoundity of the Doctrine and on the other to guarantee the amplitude of the method.

(x) The scheme of Dasapāramitās and Dasabhūmis is another salient feature of Mahāyāna. The Mahāyānists contend that there are certain spiritual aspirants who by developing *bodhicitta* (thought of enlightenment) and by fulfilling the ten Perfections (Dasapāramitās) and by ascending the ten stages of Bodhisatva's career attain the summum bonum of Buddha-hood. *Mahāyāna-*

Sūtra works such as the *Laṅkāvatāra* and the *Daśabhūmika Sūtras;* Śāstra works such as *Mahāyāna Sūtrālaṅkāra* and *Bodhisattva bhūmi* furnish details of the scheme of progressive spiritual advancement of a Bodhisattva by the practice of ten virtues or *pāramitās* (perfections) such as charity (*dāna*), precepts (*śīla*), forbearance (*kṣānti*), energy (*vīrya*), meditation (*dhyāna*) and wisdom (*prajñā*), skilful means (*upāya-kauśalya*) vow (*praṇidhāna*), Strength or power (*bala*) and knowledge (*jñāna*).

(xi) The conception of the ten stages of spiritual growth of a Bodhisattva is another unique feature of Mahāyāna. The ten stages of a Bodhisattva's career are (a) the joyful (*pramudita*), (b) immaculate (*vimalā*), (c) the illuminating (*prabhākarī*), (d) the radiant (*arciṣmatī*), (e) difficult to conquer (*sudurjayā*), (f) face-to-face to bodhi (*abhimukhi*), (g) far-going (*dūraṅgamā*), immovable (*acalā*), (h) good thought (*sādhumatī*), and (i) cloud of the law (*dharma meghā*).

(xii) Mahāyāna Pantheon model of worship and Monastic life: With the Mahāyāna development of doctrines of bodhisattva, Trikāya a well-defined and classified pantheon, concepts of heavens and hells came into existence. In Mahāyāna Tāntric Buddhism the male and female deities are depicted as the personfications of *upāya* (skillful means) and *prajñā* (wisdom).

(xiii) As regards the Mahāyāna monistic life, it gives increased importance to a dedicated household life. Having followed the general rules of Theravāda in their monastic life, modifying some of them according to their needs, the Mahāyānists added certain additional monastic features of their own such as having a spiritual guide (*kalyāṇa mitra*), learning the ways of good conduct (*bhadracariya*), entreating the Buddha to be the guides of all beings, etc. Throwing light on the salient features of Mahāyāna, noted Indian historian and Buddhalogist Prof. G.C. Pandey rightly observes:

> The real Buddha as supernatural and gracious Being, the *dharma* as the intuitable but inconceivable and ineffable Absolute, the identifiability of the canon by its conformity to truth, the spiritual quest as the quest for the absolute well-being of all, the reality of mystical secret or ahistoric tradition, the possibility of non-verbal communication, the multiplicity of superhuman saviors ultimately channelling the grace of Buddha, the pre-eminence of altruism, compassion and love among moral virtues, these are some of the major features which give Mahāyāna its distinctive character.[19]

Points of Agreement Between Theravāda and Mahāyāna

Basically Mahāyāna was in consonance with the spirit of Lord Buddha's teachings. G.C. Pandey affirms[20] that the original Buddhism which is neither clearly Hīnayānic nor clearly Mahāyānic contains the seeds of both. Since Theravāda (i.e., Hīnayāna) was the older historical tradition of Buddhism Mahāyāna did not totally reject the former. According to Sir Charles Eliot,[21] Mahāyāna ideas are found in Pāli Nikāyas of the *Sutta Piṭaka* either as mere seeds or as well-grown plants and between Theravāda and Mahāyāna there was (only) a great difference in emphasis. G.C. Pande holds[22] that Mahāyāna shares with Theravāda (Hīnayāna) the emphasis on

19. *Ibid.*, p. 11.
20. *Ibid.*, p. 7.
21. See B.L Suzuki, *Mahāyāna Buddhism*, p. 35.
22. G.C. Pande, *op. cit.*, p. 11.

selflessness, to abandon egoism and attachment to sensual pleasures, adherence to law of *karma* and to do good and avoid evil in accordance with the law of discipline. In Saṅghrakshita's view[23] Theravāda, Mahāyāna and Tantrayāna are the three successively higher stages of a single Path. All Mahāyāna doctrines can be discovered in germinal form in the Theravāda *Tripiṭaka*. While throwing light on the similarity between Theravāda and Mahāyāna Buddhism, Nalinaksha Dutt[24] brings out the following five points of agreement between the two branches of Buddhism:

1. According to both, there are three basic characteristics of existence, viz. that all phenomena in a state of suffering (*dukkha*) are transient (*anitya*) and momentary (*kṣanika*); and are devoid of real substance (*anātmakam*).
2. Both agree on the universal validity of the Law of causation (*pratītya-samutpāda*).
3. Both agree that the world has neither beginning nor an end.
4. According to both, it is essential to realize the Four Noble Truths (*catur-ārya-satyās*).
5. Both emphasize the Buddha's teaching to get rid of lust, hatred and delusion (*rāga, dveṣa and moha*).

The Principal Differences Between Theravāda and Mahāyāna

(i) According to Asaṅga's *Mahāyāna Sūtrālaṅkāra*, there are five differences between Śrāvakayāna and Mahāyāna in their objective, teaching, application, way of life and time. Whereas Theravāda canonical scriptures are

---

23. Bhikshu Saṅgharakshita, *op. cit.*, p. 261.
24. Nalinaksha Dutt, *Mahāyāna Buddhism*, p. 82.

written in Pāli, the early and later Mahāyāna writings are in hybrid Sanskrit and Sanskrit. In Theravāda perspective Buddha is a historical person who shows the path of salvation and remains merely as the pointer of the path. In Mahāyāna, the Buddha is not only the discoverer of the path but also depicted as the living ideal, the inspirer and the object of contemplation.

(ii) Scholars like H. Nakamura, G.C. Pande, Bhikshu Saṅgharakshita, Nalinaksha Dutt bring out the points of difference between the two schools which are as follows: Whereas Theravāda is ethical and historical Mahāyāna is religious and metaphysical. Whereas the relic worship is more common in Theravāda, image-worship is more common in Mahāyāna. Whereas, Theravāda lays stress only on self-ethics and self-discipline, Mahāyāna emphasizes self-sacrifice and soteriology or the doctrine of salvation through the Buddha and Bodhisattvas. While both Theravāda and Mahāyāna contain philosophy and religion, Mahāyāna contains more metaphysics. Being quite similar to Hindu sectarian religions such as theistic religion of Vaiṣṇavism, Mahāyāna is closer to Hinduism than Theravāda. In Theravāda, Tantra has no place whereas it is an important branch of Mahāyāna.

(iii) As distinguished from the Theravāda individualistic goal of *nirvāṇa,* which is attained by the annihilation of lust, hatred and delusion and realization of the Four Noble Truths resulting in the peaceful and blissful state, the Mahāyāna objective is the attainment of perfect knowledge (*prajñāpāramitā*) of the Buddha. In contrast to the spiritual individualism of Theravāda, which is the basic criterion that differentiates it from Mahāyāna, the latter evolves the unbounded altruistic ideal of the Bodhisattva (as opposed to selfish goal of

Śrāvakās and Pratyekabuddhas). When compared to the goal of Śrāvakās in Theravāda, the goal of Bodhisattvas in Mahāyāna is the Tathāgata-knowledge (*tathāgatajñāna*), which is the highest truth (*paramārtha-satya*).

(iv) In contrast to the Theravāda objective of the realization of the non-existence of soul, viz. *Pudgala-nairātmya* by means of the eradication of mental and physical impurities (*kleśāvaraṇam*), the Mahāyāna aims at not only *Pudgala-nairātmya*, but also the *dharma-nairātmya* (emptiness of all elements) by means of eradication of obscurations (*jñeyāvaraṇam*).

(v) Although both Theravāda and Mahāyāna accept the *Abhidhamma* classification of *dharmas*, the former regards them as realistic whereas for the latter they are unreal.

(vi) As opposed to the Theravāda negative conception of *nirvāṇa*, which is based on *Abhidhamma* conception of conditional *dharma*, which are regarded as ultimately real, the Mahāyāna explained the transcendental in terms of non-existence and non-entity. Whereas Hīnayāna schools in general and Theravāda in particular lay stress on the empirical and phenomenal standpoint which culminate in *Abhidhamma*, the Mahāyāna emphasize the noumenal and absolutistic standpoint which is implicit in the concepts of *nirvāṇa*, *pratītyasamutpāda* and *vijñāna*.

(vii) Where as the Theravādins stressed upon the first series of the doctrine of causality (*paṭiccasamuppāda*), which represents a process of estimation of ignorance, the Mahāyānists concentrated on the second series of law of dependent origination, which positively depict *nirvāṇa* in terms of growth and development.

(viii) Similarly as opposed to Theravāda who negatively interpreted the doctrine of Noble eight-fold path (*Ariya Aṭṭhaṅgika Magga*) for instance "right speech" as abstention from lying, harsh language, tale bearing, etc. the Mahāyāna followers, i.e., Bodhisattvas lay emphasis on the positive aspect of the eight-fold Path and practice of the Pāramitās.

(ix) As opposed to Theravāda, which is scholastic, which emphasizes on theoretical analysis and classification of physical and mental states, Mahāyāna is speculative.

(x) In contrast to the Theravāda, which is conservative and literal-minded, Mahāyāna adheres to the spirit of Buddha's teaching rather than the letter. Whereas, the Theravādins' slavish dependence on the letter of the teaching resulted in an almost evacuation of the spirit, the anti-literalism of the Mahāyāna consists in its vigorous and systematic application of the truth variously designated as *nirvāṇa, tathatā, śūnyatā* and *dharmakāya*.

(xi) Unlike the Theravādins who identified the Truth with conceptual formulations as well as equated them with their verbal expression, the Mahāyānists regarded the verbal expressions of Buddha's teaching as merely symbolic indication and considered *dharma* as only a raft, which serves us just as an instrument to realize truth. Thus like Theravādins, Mahāyānists have not mistaken "rational comprehension" of the Buddha's teaching for its actual realization.

(xii) The Theravāda and Mahāyāna respectively represent the centripetal and centrifugal tendencies in Buddha's teaching. While the centripetal tendency of Theravāda prevents disintegration, the centrifugal tendency of Mahāyāna preserves from petrification. Thus, by exerting over the doctrines and methods of Buddhism Theravāda and Mahāyāna maintain an absolute equilibrium before literalising and the liberalizing influences on which depends the very existence of Buddhism.

(xiii) As against Mahāyāna, Theravāda lays undue emphasis on the formal aspects of monasticism and gives predominance to the institutional aspects of religion. The Mahāyānists strengthened the monastic ideal by drawing distinction between spiritual and monastic life.

5

Theravāda Buddhist Classics

DHAMMAPADA

Introduction

The *Dhammapada* is given almost an unique place in Theravāda Buddhist literature. It forms a part of the Pāli Buddhist Canon, though its exact place is disputable. However, as one of the religious classics of the world, it was accepted at the council of Aśoka held in 240 or 247 BC, as the Buddha's original teaching. Even before that since the period of the first Buddhist council (477 BC), which settled the canon the *Dhammapada* was believed to be the "utterances of Buddha himself." It is an anthology of verses, which is the most popular of *Tripiṭaka*. Albert J. Edmunds calls it in his introduction to the edition of *Dhammapada* as an "immortal classic of Asia."[1]

In the first half of the 5th century CE, Buddhaghoṣa the celebrated commentator on Pāli *Tripiṭaka* had written a commentary called *Dhammapada Aṭṭhakathā* in Pāli language. The original recension of the Pāli text on the *Dhammapada* reached China in the 3 *c.* CE. It was translated from the Chinese by Samuel Beal into English in 1878. Beal holds that there are four principal translations of the *Dhammapada* in Chinese dated 223 CE, 345 CE, 410 CE. and 8th or 9th century CE respectively.

---

1. U. *Dhāmmajoti*, (tr.), *The Dhammapada*, Introduction, p. 1.

This famous work has been translated by different scholars of different countries in different languages. Fausball translated this work in Latin, which was published in 1855. Weber and Hu translated the *Dhammapada* respectively in German and French. Later the *Dhammapada* was translated into English by renowned scholars like P.L. Vaidya, Max Müller in 1870, James Gray in 1881, F.L. Woodward in 1921; J.P. Cooke in 1890; Ceylonese scholars such as Narada, A.P. Buddhadatta and Indian Scholars like Rādhākriṣnan, Kunhan Raja, and Buddharakkita. Some of the unpublished translations of this work by scholars like G.P. Malalasekera and Anand Maitreya are also available in manuscript form. In twentieth century among Indian languages there are atleast one Hindi and eight Telugu translations of the *Dhammapada*.[2]

The title of *Dhammapada* has been interpreted in various ways because of the ambiguity and the multifaceted meanings the word emits. The word *Dhamma* has many meanings such as "discipline," "law," "religion," etc. The word *pada* also has several meanings. In the ancient Pāli lexicon *Abhidhānappadīpikā*,[3] it is explained as "place," "protection," "*nirvāṇa*," "cause," "word," "thing," "portion," "foot or footstep," etc. It has been translated by different scholars in various ways such as "the footsteps of religion" "sentences of religion" "a collection of verses," "verses on *dharma*," "the word of Buddha" "The Path of Virtue" and so on and so forth. For example: this title was first rendered by Gogerly as "The foot steps of religion"[4] "Fausboll[5] translated it as "a collection

2. V.V.S. Saibaba, Dhammapadamu, *Journal of Telugu Studies*, vol. I no. 1, March, 1988, pp. 128-29.

3. Swamy Dwarakadas Shastri (ed.), *Abhidhānappadīpikā and Ekākkhara Kośa*, pp. 4, 16, 49, 142.

4. U. *Dhammajoti, op. cit.*, p. i.

5. F. Max Müller (tr.) *The Dhammapada*, See. Introduction IV, p. 55.

of verses on religion." Samuel Beal is of the opinion that the Chinese seem to have taken *Dhammapada* in the sense of "scriptural texts or stanzas of law."[6] *Dhammajoti* translated it as a collection of verses from the "teachings of the Buddha."[7]

The *Dhammapada* consists of twenty-six chapters, which comprises of four hundred and twenty-three verses. In the view of K.J. Saunders[8] this work depicts the "religious life" of the days of Buddha. It conveys the very spirit of the Buddha who preached to practise the life of contemplation and stimulating mind-culture. Mostly the *Dhammapada* consists of precepts acceptable to all Indian religions. Scholars like B.C. Law have pointed[9] out that similar ethical notions are found in Upaniṣads like the *Chāndogya*, the *Kaṭhā* and in the *Manū-śaṁhitā, Mahābhārata*, and *Bhagavad-Gītā*; Jain classics like *Uttarādhyayana* and *Sūtrakṛtāṅga* and also Tamil works like *Tirukkural*. In support of the translation of the title *Dhammapada* as stanzas of law we find in it principal doctrines of Buddhism namely the four "Noble Truths," the "Middle Way," the eight-fold path, etc.

The *Dhammapada* comprises some of the following important ideas: we come across in it the statements of common sense. It is stated in this work that true monks are found only in Buddhist order and the path which leads to *nirvāṇa* is the only way to salvation or liberation from Saṁsāra. "*Dhamma* or Righteousness is the driving principle of the universe. Insight into *dhamma* is enlightenment. According to the *Dhammapada*, there are no eternal things." The non-

6. Samuel Beal, (tr.) *Dhammapada*, p. 1.
7. U. *Dhammajoti, op. cit.*, Introduction, p. iii.
8. W.D.C. Wagiswara and K.J. Saunders (tr.) *The Buddha's Way of Virtue*, see Introduction, p. 11.
9. B.C. Law, *Some Thoughts on the Buddhist Dhammapada in Āryan Path*, vol-XXXIV, no. 3, March, 1965.

permanence of things is repeatedly emphasized in this book. Freedom from multiplicity is also asserted in this work. *Avidyā* or ignorance is stated as the greatest taint and escape from it leads one to *nirvāṇa*. One of the main teachings of the *Dhammapada* is that one should totally abandon the *taṇhā* and should completely free himself to disentangle from the chains of rebirth. According to the *Dhammapada*, a *bhikṣu* should guard his senses, cultivate contentment, strictly observe the rules of the order; he should associate himself with beneficent friends and should lead pure life.

The nature of *nirvāṇa* is spoken of in a variety of ways in this treatise. It is described as the "other shore" towards which one should endeavour to reach by crossing the realm of death. In some places it is also described as void (*śūnya*) the signless (*animitta*) and deliverance (*mokṣa*). It is further characterised as the unconditioned life of bliss (*sukha*), the ineffable (*anakhata*) and the untrodden land (*agatam disam*). The *Dhammapada* exhorts the aspirants through a number of graphic similes to be away from the sensuous world, and to reach the goal of *nirvāṇa*, by the practice of *dharma*. As K.J. Saunders rightly observes that:

> the spirit of Buddha can be seen in *Dhammapada*[10] which contains the concentrated essence of religion.

Venerable or Arhat

An *arhat* is he who has reached the highest degree of the four orders of Āryas namely "Stream enterer" (*sotāpanna*), "once-returner" (*sakrdagāmin*), non-returner (*anāgāmin*) and *arhat*. Just as swans who leave their lake, the *arhat*s abandon their home and fixed abode being thoughtful and always exerting. An *arhat* perceives unconditional freedom, under-

10. W.D.C. Wagiswara and K.J. Saunders, *op. cit.*, Introduction, p. 9.

stands the signless void. The path of an *arhat* who has attained *nirvāṇa* is invisible, incomprehensible like the path of the birds in the air or of fishes in the water. A wakeful *arhat* is aware of his own salvation without forgetting that *saṁsāra* is full of suffering, impermanent and unreal. Here his endeavour denotes the spiritual activity. An *arhat* is one whose passions are rooted out, who is tolerant, who does his duty and lives in purity.

Being indifferent in all duality an *arhat* lives as firm as threshold or the thunderbolt of Indra, as patient as the earth and as pure and serene as mudless undisturbed lake. He is calm in mind, speech and action. He knows the uncreated (*akata*) i.e., *nirvāṇa*. He has put an end to all occasions for performing good or bad actions. He is regarded as the best of all men (*uttama puruṣa*) and exalted.

> The man, who is not credulous, who understands the uncreate (*nibbāna*) who has cut off the link, who has put an end to occasion (of good and evil), who has vomited all desires, — he, indeed is the noblest of men.[11]

He is happy wherever he is whether it is a hamlet or a forest or a sea or dry land. He does not look for sensual pleasures. Therefore wherever the *arhat* stays it is a happy place.

Awakened or the Buddha

In Buddhist tradition the word *buddha* is not to be understood as a proper name of a person but denotes the completely awakened or enlightened spiritual personalities. The Buddha or the Enlightened one is a supremely awakened personality. He is like a King of Kings (*chakravartin*). The Buddha's domain is spiritual and moral but not secular. In this sense the Buddha

---

11. Narada Maha There (tr.) *The Dhammapada*, p. 69, *The Dhammapada*, St. 97, See Arhat Vaggo, St. 8.

is the King of Righteousness (*dharma rāja*) and a conqueror (*jina*), who has attained victory over passions. There is no one equal to him in the world. The Buddha is imperceptible (*anantagocara*). He possesses infinite perception. His vision is boundless. He is trackless (*apada*). In other words he defies all description. There is no possibility for him to slide again into empirical existence. The Buddha is superior to all god-folk. Even the gods have a longing to attain the state of Buddhahood. The summary of the teaching of the Buddha is to abstain from all evil, to do good and to purify one's mind.

> *sabba pāpassa akaranam kusalassa upasampadā,*
> *sacittapariyodapanaṁ etaṁ buddhāna sāsanaṁ.*

> Not to do any evil, to cultivate good,
> To purify one's mind, this is the advice of the Buddha's[12]

Thus, the Buddhist ideal is not merely negative as it is often supposed. Human birth and mortal life is a hard accomplishment. Similarly it is difficult to have the occasion to hear the Law (*dhamma*). The arising of the Buddha is also a rare phenomenon.

> Hard is birth as man, Hard is the life of mortals, Hard is the hearing of the sublime truth, Hard is the appearance of the Buddhas[13]

The true follower of the Buddha should not blame others. He should cultivate restraint. He should not hurt or molest others. Thus for the Buddha forbearance is the highest penance and *nibbāna* is the best of things. The advice of all Buddhas is to strictly observe the Pāṭimokkha rules, i.e., moderation in eating, dwelling in solitude and diligence in meditation. The Buddha further preached the importance of rooting out the craving for earthly as well as celestial pleasures.

---

12. *Ibid.*, p. 133, *The Dhammapada*, St. 183, Buddha Vaggo, Verse. 5.
13. *Ibid.*, *The Dhammapada*, St. 182, Buddha Vaggo, Verse. 4.

When human beings are threatened by fear they seek refuge of various kinds such as mountains, forests, dwellings of ascetics and tree-shrines. But none of these refuges is secure or supreme because one cannot free himself from suffering by taking refuge in any of the above. There is only one safe and best refuge for humanity namely, *tri-saraṇā* (triple refuge) namely the Buddha, the *dhamma*, the *saṅgha.* By going to these triple refuges one perceives clearly the four noble truths and their constituents by right understanding. The safe and best refuge for mankind is the knowledge of the four Noble Truths and the eight-fold Noble Path, which leads one to the cessation of suffering and delivers from all sorrow and pain.

The Buddha is a blessed being. He is a supernormal person and the Exalted one who rarely arises in this world and wherever such a one is born that household attains happiness. So the appearance of the Buddha, his preaching of the True Law, the Unity of the Order and the spiritual effort of the united members of the Order (*saṅgha*) all these are happy phenomena. Those who revere and pay homage to the Buddha or his disciples who have overcome evil, free from all fear, transcend sorrow and find deliverance by their attainment of *nirvāṇa*, acquire great and immeasurable merit.

Way or Magga

The Path or the way in which the technical term used for the noble eight-fold path evidently refers to the title of *Dhammapada.* This way constitutes the way to the cessation of suffering (*duḥkha nirodha mārga*), the last of the four Noble Truths.

The Noble eight-fold Path (*āriya aṭṭhangika magga*) is the best of all paths. The four Noble Truths are the best of all truths. Passionlessness is the best of all virtues. The Seer or the Buddha is best of all mankind. This is the only path that leads a spiritual aspirant to purify one's vision and which confounds the Māra. The Buddha is called as the "great remover of thorns." He showed this path by which an aspirant will put an end to sufferings. The Buddha who understood the way to the removal of the point of arrow or the thorns in the flesh indicated the way by which one can overcome the *dukkha*. The Buddha or all the Buddhas should be understood only as preachers and pointers of the path. Those who strive on the path being thoughtful will be freed from the Māra's bondage. The path of purity can be obtained by an aspirant, who realizes that all conditioned things are impermanent, full of suffering and substanceless. One cannot find the path of wisdom if he is slothful, lazy, whose mind is full of inertia and who do not exert at the right time. An aspirant should cultivate restraint in one's thought, speech and action, which enables him to achieve the path. One has to strive to increase wisdom or knowledge because meditation gives rise to knowledge and lack of meditation leads to the loss of wisdom.

> Indeed, from meditation does wisdom spring, without meditation wisdom wanes: — Knowing this two-fold path of gain and loss let him so conduct himself such that wisdom may increase.[14]

The Buddha exhorted the *bhikkhus* to cut down the entire forest of lust, not merely the tree of desire, which will enable them to completely get rid of suffering. So long as even a single desire such as lust towards women is not severed, one's mind clings to phenomenal existence just as a suckling calf is attached to its mother.

---

14. *Ibid.*, p. 211, *The Dhammapada*, St. 282, Magga Vaggo, Verse. 10.

> For as long as the slightest brushwood (of passion) of man towards women, is not cut down, so long is his mind in bondage, like the milch calf unto the mother cow.[15]

An aspirant should cut off one's craving or love of self like one who removes the autumn lotus with the hand. One has to cultivate the path of peace in order to reach the goal of *nibbāna* showed by the Buddha. Without thinking of the death, the fool meditates discriminating that he lives in rainy season or in a winter season. The mind of a person which is intoxicated with attachment to his children and cattle, is seized and is carried off by death, just as a great flood washes off a sleeping village. Neither one's relations, nor kinsfolk can help a person who is overtaken by death. Hence a wise man who understands this path should make his way clear towards the goal of *nibbāna*.

Mendicant or Bhikkhu

The cardinal virtue of a monk is to use restraint in all the five senses: eye, nose, ear, tongue and body. A monk who has control over his senses, mind and speech, who delights in meditation, who lives in solitude, composed and contented, is free from all misery. A monk's speech is sweet for he speaks wisely and calmly and teaches the Law and its meaning. A monk does not fall off from True Law or sublime doctrine because he abides in the *dhamma*, follows it, contemplates on it and does not deviate from it.

> The *bhikkhu* who dwells in the *dhamma*, who delights in the *dhamma*, who meditates on the *dhamma*, who well remembers the *dhamma*, does not fall away from the *dhamma* sublime.[16]

A monk does not obtain peace of mind if he despises his own gain and envies at others' gains. Even the gods praise a monk

---

15. *Ibid.*, p. 213, *The Dhammapada*, St. 284, Magga Vaggo, Verse. 12.
16. *Ibid.*, p. 273, *The Dhammapada*, St. 364, Bhikkhu Vaggo, Verse. 5.

who is pure in livelihood and is not slothful. In other words, a *bhikkhu* should extinguish craving. A monk who does not identify himself with name and form realizing that they are unreal, who lives in friendliness, contemplates on universal love (*metta*), who delights in the Buddha's teachings attains the blissful state of *nirvāṇa* which is the cessation of all conditioned things.

> He who has no "I" and "me" (conception) whatever towards mind and body, he who grieves not for that which he has not, — he, indeed is called a Bhikkhu.[17]

A monk should empty the boat or ship by casting off lust and hatred so as to enable it to proceed swiftly to *nirvāṇa*. A *bhikkhu* should cut off the five bonds or fetters namely, belief in self, doubt, indulgence in wrongful rites and ceremonies, sense-desires and enmity. A *bhikkhu* should get rid off the five undesirable things, namely craving for the realm of forms and formlessness, conceit, self-will and ignorance. Besides, he should cultivate the five faculties or psychical powers namely faith, energy, mindfulness, concentration and wisdom. A monk who has overcome the "five" fetters namely, lust, hatred, delusion, conceit and false views, is one who has crossed the flood of rebirth. A monk should not be passive but must be vigilant and should be active. He is advised not to be negligent and not to allow his mind to whirl on sensual pleasures and thereby suffers the pangs of hell of flames. Meditation and wisdom are correlated and inter-dependent. One does not exist devoid of another. A *bhikkhu* who realizes their togetherness and that both are essential for *nirvāṇa* attains his goal soon.

> There is no concentration to him who lacks wisdom, nor is there wisdom to him who lacks concentration. In whom are

17. *Ibid.*, p. 275, *The Dhammapada*, St. 367, Bhikkhu Vaggo, Verse. 8.

> both concentration and wisdom — he indeed, is in the presence of *nibbāna*.[18]

A *bhikkhu* who dwells in solitude, whose mind is tranquil, who clearly sees the Law will experience joy of those who attain the immortal *nirvāṇa*. By knowing the origin and destruction of the elements of the body that they are in a constant flux, a monk realizes bliss or the nectar of immorality. A wise monk should begin to conduct his life by guarding his senses, by cultivating contentment by observing the precepts of the law and by associating with noble friends who lead a zealous and pure life. A monk who is cordial and abandons evil in his behaviour makes an end of suffering.

A *bhikkhu* is admonished to give up lust and hatred similar to a jasmine plant, which sheds its withered flowers. A monk who has controlled his thoughts, speech and action, who has renounced all worldliness is known as "tranquilised." "A monk should rouse himself, guard himself and examine himself and such a one lives in a happy state." No one else can do this because the self is a lord of self; self is the refuge of self.

> By self do you censure yourself? By self do you examine yourself? Self-guarded and mindful, O *bhikkhu*, you shall live happily.[19]

Hence a mendicant should curb one's self just as a merchant curbs a noble horse.

> Self, indeed, is the saviour of self. Self, indeed, is one's refuge, control, therefore, your own self as a merchant, a noble stead.[20]

---

18. *Ibid.*, p. 279, *The Dhammapada*, St. 372, Bhikkhu Vaggo, Verse. 13.
19. *Ibid.*, p. 283, *The Dhammapada*, St. 379, Bhikkhu Vaggo, Verse. 20.
20. *Ibid.*, p. 285, *The Dhammapada*, St. 380, Bhikkhu Vaggo, Verse. 21.

A monk full of joy with faith in Buddha's doctrine attains the peaceful state which is the cessation of *saṁskāras* and which is the blissful end of the cycle of transmigration.

SUTTA-NIPĀTA

Introduction

The *Sutta-Nipāta* belongs to the *Khuddhakanikāya* of the *Suttapiṭaka*. It is a very ancient teaching of the Buddha and contains an authentic doctrine. It is earlier than the *Dhammapada*. It consists of five chapters (*vaggas*), viz. Uragavagga, Cūlāvagga, Mahāvagga, Aṭṭhakavagga and Pārāyaṇavagga. The *Sutta-Nipāta* is translated into English by renowned scholars like Lord Chalmers into verse (1932) and V. Fausboll into prose (1968). The Pāli Text Society of England published a commentary on the *Sutta-Nipāta* known as a *Paramaṭṭhajotikā* edited by Helmer Smith in romanised character, which contains rich materials useful for the reconstruction of the ancient Indian history.

Scholars like M. Winternitz , B.C. Law, Lord Chalmers, V. Fausboll and Oliver Abeynayake threw light on the antiquity of the five cantoes of the older and the present versions of the *Sutta-Nipāta*. R.O. Franke holds that the *Sutta-Nipāta* is a collection made up of earlier and later texts and is certainly not a unified work.[21] While referring to R. Otto Franke, Winternitz observes single *sutta*s and numerous *gāthā*s from all the five cantoes of the *Sutta-Nipāta* can be traced to other texts of the Pāli canon.[22] As regards the chronology of this treatise Oliver Abeynayake holds that the discourses of the *Sutta-Nipāta* prior to their incorporation into separate text did

21. M. Winternitz, *A History of Indian Literature*, vol. II, p. 98 fn. 3.
22. *Ibid.*, p. 92 fn. 4.

exist either as distinct poems or as part of the early canonical texts since out of the thirty-eight discourses of the first three cantoes of the text, viz. *Uragavagga, Cūlāvagga* and *Mahāvagga* twelve *sutta*s are found in other canonical texts namely the *Majjhima*, the *Saṁyutta Nikāya*s and the three works of the *Khuddaka Nikāya*, viz. the *Khuddakapāṭha*, the *Apadāna* and the *Jātaka*.[23] For example the *Khuddakapāṭha* contains three *suttas*[24] of the *Sutta-Nipāta*, viz. the *Maṅgala Sutta*, the *Ratana Sutta* and the *Metta Sutta*s. King Aśoka's Bhabru Edict refers to the three *sutta*s which belong to the *Sutta-Nipāta* among the texts recommended for study.[25] According to Winternitz, the *sutta*s which belong to the *Sutta-Nipāta* are highly esteemed as "works of poetic art" and its popularity is evident from its frequent occurrence in Buddhist literature.[26] Scholars like Lamotte also subscribing to this view contend that more than half of the discourses of the *Sutta-Nipāta* are referred to in the Indian Buddhist literary works,[27] viz. the *Saṁyuttāgama*, the *Divyāvadāna*, the *Mahāvastu*, the *Vibhāśa*, the *Abhidharma Kośa*, the *Prajñāpāramitopadeśa* and the *Bodhisattvabhūmi*.

The compositions of the *Aṭṭhaka* and the *Pārāyaṇa Vagga*s can be traced as far back as to the lifetime of the Buddha since they were quoted during his life and owing to their existence as independent treatises prior to their incorporation in the *Sutta-Nipāta* as a seperate text, these fourth and fifth cantoes can be said to have belonged to the oldest stratum of Pāli canon.[28] As regards their antiquity, the *Aṭṭhaka* and the *Pārāyaṇa*

23. O. Abeynayake, *A Textual and Historical Analysis of the Khuddaka-Nikāya*, pp. 135-36.
24. M. Winternitz, *op. cit.*, p. 78, fn. 1.
25. *Ibid.*, vol. II, p. 93.
26. *Ibid.*
27. O. Abeynayake, *op. cit.*, p. 139.
28. *Ibid.*, p. 44 fn. 3, *ibid.*, p. 75.

Vaggas also have been quoted in the *Vinaya Piṭaka*, the *Saṁyutta* and the *Aṅguttara Nikāyas* of the Pāli canon and since they also precede their canonical commentary, viz. *Niddesa* they are regarded as the earliest elements of the *Sutta-Nipāta*.[29] All the *suttas* of the fourth and fifth cantoes of the *Sutta-Nipāta* are equally old[30] and since very early times the two *vaggas* have been known to the then Buddhist community as two distinct texts.[31] They together form the subject matter of the old commentary known as *Niddesa*.[32] We may infer from the non-mentioning of the name *Sutta-Nipāta* anywhere in *Niddesa* that the *Aṭṭhaka* and the *Pārāyaṇa Vaggas* were the two distinct texts composed earlier than the present form of the *Sutta-Nipāta* available to us. Moreover owing to their absence in the *Niddesa* we can infer with certainity that by the time of the composition of the *Niddesa* the first three cantoes of the *Sutta-Nipāta*, viz. *Uragavagga*, *Cūlavagga* and *Mahāvagga* might not have been in existence and also that they were of a later origin when compared to the fourth and fifth cantoes.[33] The *Aṭṭhaka* and the *Pārāyaṇa Vaggas* have been recorded in the Mahāsaṅghika's *Dharmagupta vinaya*[34] and the *Saṁyuttāgama*.[35] Other Buddhist works, viz. the *Abhidharma-mahāvibhāsā* and the *Vinayamātṛka* refer to the last two cantoes of the *Sutta-Nipāta*.[36]

---

29. Lord Chalmers, (tr.) *Buddha's Teachings Being the Sutta-Nipāta or Discourse-Collection*, Introduction, p. xviii, O. Abeynayake, *op. cit.* p. 75, fn. 2.
30. O. Abeynayake, *op. cit.*, p. 77.
31. *Ibid.*, p. 80.
32. *Ibid.*, p. 67.
33. B.C. Law, *History of Pāli Literature*, vol. I, p. 233.
34. O Abeynayake, *op. cit.*, p. 41.
35. *Ibid.*, p. 139.
36. O Abeynayake, *op. cit.*, p. 75, fn. 6.

As one of the oldest books of the Pāli canon and from the viewpoints of its language, style as well as its contents the *Sutta-Nipāta* contains important traces of primitive Buddhism.[37] Fausboll also contends[38] that we come across in the contents of the *Sutta-Nipāta* an important contribution to the right understanding of primitive Buddhism, which constitute the first germs of Buddhist doctrine. Winternitz too holds[39] that by virtue of their language as well as subject matter some portions of the *Sutta-Nipāta* can be said to have belonged to the beginning stages of Buddhism and many *sutta*s seem to have originated as early as during the life-time of Buddha's first disciples. According to Fausboll,[40] from the viewpoints of language as well as its contents the greater part of the *Mahāvagga*, the whole of the *Aṭṭhakavagga* and some portions of the *Uragavagga* are very old. The language of the *Sutta-Nipāta* indicates that some of its portions are far older than the *Dhammapada*. This is because the metres of this treatise resemble the Vedic metres of eight syllables (*Anuṣṭhubh*), eleven syllables (*Triṣṭhubh*) or twelve syllables (*Jagati*). A combination of *Indravajra* and *Upendravajra* or *Vaṁsastha* and *Indravaṁsa*, *Gana* and *Matra vrittas*, stanzas in *Vaitāliya* and *Aupacchandasika* metres appear in this work.[41]

We come across Vedic and Epic type of "Old riddle-poetry" in the *Āḷavaka Sutta* of the *Uragavagga* (I.10) and the *Sūciloma Sutta* of *Cūlavagga* (II.5) of the *Sutta-Nipāta*[42] wherein by presenting Buddhist ethical doctrines a Sage answers a

37. B.C. Law, *op. cit.*, p. 238.
38. V. Fausboll (tr.), *The Sutta-Nipāta*, Introduction, p. xii.
39. M. Winternitz, *op. cit.*, p. 93.
40. V. Fausboll, *op. cit.*, Introduction, p. xi.
41. B.C. Law, *op. cit.*, p. 234.
42. Lord Chalmers, *op. cit.*, pp. 44-47, 66-69.

Yakṣa's riddles similar to the Yudhiṣṭhira-Yakṣa dialogue in the *Mahābhārata*. Besides the above didactic dialogues, we find a few narrative dialogues in the three *sutta*s of the *Mahāvagga* of the *Sutta-Nipāta*,[43] viz. *Pabbajjā Sutta*, the *Padhāna Sutta*, and the *Nālaka Sutta* which can be cited as fine specimens of the ancient ballad poetry. About one-third of the poems of the *Sutta-Nipāta* belong to the category of ballad poetry. In this collection some of its verses contain the Buddha's dialogues with others and some narrate the short incidents. A few ancient ballads of the *Sutta-Nipāta*[44] consist of the reliable records of the Buddha's life as well as the earliest beginnings of the Buddha legend. For instance the above referred three *sutta*s of the *Mahāvagga* despite their legendary features and mythical character furnish the simple account of Buddha's life and which probably had served as the seed-bed of the epic version of the Buddha's life. Of these three *sutta*s of the *Mahāvagga* the *Nālaka Sutta* narrates the events soon after Gautama Buddha's birth; the *Pabbajjā Sutta* provides an account of his great departure from home to homeless state (*Mahābhiniskramaṇa*); and the *Padhāna Sutta* portrays Māra's endeavours to dissuade Gautama Buddha from his objective of attaining Buddhahood and the former's defeat by the latter.

Central Teachings

The *Sutta-Nipāta* contains information about the socio-economic conditions of India in the days of Gautama Buddha. It shows the division of Indian society into two large and distinguished sects namely śramaṇas and brāhmaṇas. Śramanas are divided into four kinds and brāhmaṇas are divided into three kinds on the basis of different groups attached to different teachers at the time of the Buddha.

---

43. *Ibid.*, pp. 98-105, 164-173.

44. M. Winternitz, *op. cit.*, p. 186.

In the *Sutta-Nipāta* we come across a number of references which bear the ideas of Brāhmaṇism. For instance the *Brāhmaṇa-Dhammika Sutta* (i.e., *sutta* of the pious among the brāhmaṇas) differentiates "True Brāhmaṇism" of the ancient times in contrast to latter folk, viz. brāhmaṇas for name-sake who were allured by wealth, women and luxurious life by king of Ikshvāku. All this resulted in the deterioration of morals and intermingling of castes. The *Vāseṭṭha Sutta* enunciates that true *Brahman*-hood does not consist in birth but in good conduct. The Buddhist monk who is faithful to his vow is hailed up as the True Muni. The *Kasibhāradvāja Sutta* contains the Buddha's denial of scornful attitude of labourers, farmers and shepherds of a Buddhist monk who is depicted as "an idler" which is their misapprehension.

The *Āmagandha Sutta* contrasts the Buddhist ideal life with the Brāhmaṇic ideal in refined polemics and depicts the Buddhist ideal of life as more superior than the latter. The *sutta* further throws light on the Buddhist idea of purity of life when in response to a brāhmaṇa who regards the observance of the dietary laws as the highest moral law and the tasting of forbidden meat as the most reprehensible impurity, the Buddha exhorts that true impurity does not consist in eating meat but in violence involved in torturing living beings, murder, tyranny, theft, lies, frauds, illegitimate sexual life, unmercifulness, covetousness, etc. Thus, in contrast to Brāhmaṇical teaching the Buddha asserts that a human being is defiled by a wicked mind and actions and no outward observances can purify such a person.

The *Sutta-Nipāta* provides information about the religious conditions and philosophical views of India in the days of Gautama Buddha. The Brāhmaṇas hold that the purity comes from philosophical views, from tradition or scriptures. They were of the opinion that except by following their teachings one could not attain the Bliss or Freedom.

Even though the Buddha belongs to the śramaṇa class, he had transcended their systems. The *Sutta-Nipāta* depicts the Buddha firstly, as a "visionary" and secondly, as an "ascetic." As a visionary, Buddha has searched for truth without adopting any philosophical views, found it and saw the inward peace. He realised the *dharma* without any traditional instruction. The second great characteristic of Buddha is that he is an ascetic par excellence. This means he is a *muni* who has forsaken the world from home to homeless state having realised that the household life is full of defilements.

B.C. Law rightly observes that the essence of the *Sutta-Nipāta* is :

> to know the real nature of the world and knowing it, to lead a moral life shaking off all philosophical views whatsoever.[45]

According to this text, Buddhism is essentially an ethical system and *nirvāṇa* is its goal, which can be attained only by practising some ethical virtues, by realising the four Noble Truths and the Law of Dependent Origination. It emphasizes the notions such as renunciation, killing of *taṇhā*, abstaining from all desires, passions and material possessions. This supports the view that Buddhism is a world-negating religion (for example: *Khaggavisāṇa Sutta*). Some other *sutta*s which belong to *Pārāyaṇavagga* consist ideas like friendliness (*metta*), compassion (*karuṇā*) and imposition of all positive virtues and there by lay stress that Buddhism is a world-affirmating religion. In the *Sutta-Nipāta* the Brāhmin sacrifices and scriptures are almost denounced as useless and trivial. The ideas of unconditional freedom and fearlessness are emphasized in this work which enunciate that one should rely neither on teacher nor on scripture. In the *Sutta-Nipāta* commitment to anything is regarded as bondage. Truth cannot

45. B.C. Law, *op. cit.*, p. 237.

be understood by argumentation but only by faith (*saddhā*), is another principal teaching of this work.

The expositions of *Sutta-Nipāta* enable us to infer that Buddhism was not an established philosophical system by the time of its composition.[46] The *Sutta-Nipāta* represents the primitive or archaic stage wherein Buddhism is characterised as a simple ethical religion and as a repository of germs of ideas which later developed into a full fledged philosophical system.[47] During Buddha's lifetime the people of mid-India used to regard that the knowledge of philosophical systems result in purity of life. Denying the Brāhmaṇical and Sramanical views of religious life the Buddha refuted not only the philosophical systems, traditional knowledge, philosophical disputations, but also all kinds of virtuous works, worship, offerings and sacrifices which involve loss of life.[48] Even though the Buddha was a śramaṇa, he did not agree with the philosophical systems and the traditional knowledge of the brāhmaṇas. He denounced their view of religious life and futile disputations, which involve one again and again in fruitless argumentation.

Some of the *sutta*s (iii-ix and xi-xiii) in *Aṭṭhakavagga* of the *Sutta-Nipāta* emphasise the Buddha's teaching namely that the realisation of the "truth" is possible only when all views are destroyed and when one gives up all grasping. A true monk who endeavours for liberation should remember not to have conceptual and discursive thinking. He should not cling to any single view or *dharma*, which cannot encompass the truth as a whole. In the *Duṭṭhaṭṭhaka*, the *Suddhaṭṭhaka*, the *Paramaṭṭhaka*, the *Pasūra*, the *Māgandiya*, the *Kalahavivāda*, the

46. *Ibid.*, p. 238.

47. *Ibid.*

48. *Ibid.*, pp. 239-40.

Kulaviyūha and the *Mahāviyūha Sutta*s of the *Aṭṭhakavagga* (the book of Octades) and the *Nanda*, the *Gatukaṇṇi* and the *Bhadrāvudha Mānava Pucchā*s of the *Pārāyanavagga* (the Book of the Way-Across) the Buddha pronounces himself distinctly against philosophy or *Diṭṭhi* or *Darśana*. According to the *Sutta-Nipāta*, highest knowledge or *Prajñā* (*pañña*) is not something irrational. It can be said as supra-rational or "trans-rational." *Prajñā* is not opposed to logic (*tarka*), but transcends it. *Prajñā* yields the truth of non-duality.

In several *sutta*s of the *Sutta-Nipāta*, viz. the *Uraga Sutta*, the *Sammāparibbajaniya Sutta*, the *Māgandiya Sutta*, the *Purābheda Sutta*, the *Tuvaṭaka Sutta*, the *Attadaṇḍa Sutta*, the *Sāriputta Sutta*, the *Khaggavisāṇa Sutta* and the *Muni Sutta*, etc. the ideal life of a *bhikkhu* which is the prototype of a perfectly honest regular moral life is set forth. The *Sutta-Nipāta* furnishes the information on the life of an ideal *bhikkhu* (monk) in contrast to an ideal householder for whom it is almost impossible to lead a perfect ethical life. According to scholars like B.C. Law, the philosophical character of Buddhism as described in the *Sutta-Nipāta* is ethical. Hence a novice who joins the Buddhist Order gradually grows into a *bhikkhu* by observing all moral rules of conduct and by leading an austere and simple life.

A *bhikkhu* is exhorted by the Buddha to subdue his desire for name and form, taste, smell and touch, etc. He should not utter slander against others. He should live in this world like a "water-drop" on a lotus[49] without clinging to material things. A *bhikkhu* should cultivate detachment from all his relative folk and worldly possessions. He should not live subservient to anybody else. He should not deal with gold and silver by way of buying and selling it. He should scrupulously observe all the *Pāṭimokkha* rules and cultivate restraint in thought,

---

49. *Ibid.*, p. 236.

speech and action.[50] A *bhikkhu* should follow a "middle path" without indulging himself in the two extremes of worldly pleasures and self-mortification. A *bhikkhu* should realize the three cardinal principles of the Buddhist doctrine that, all phenomena involve suffering (*dukkha*), impermanence (*aniccā*) and unsubstantiality (*anattā*).[51] In the *Dhaniya Sutta* (I.2) of the *Uragavagga*, the mundane prosperity and domestic happiness of a rich owner of herds is contrasted with the homeless and absolutely passion-free peace and quietitude of the Buddha. The goal of a *bhikkhu* is arahanthood or *Nibbāna* which can be attained by perfecting oneself in the above ethical virtues by realizing the Four Noble Truths and the Law of Causation.[52] The essence of the *Sutta-Nipāta* as enjoined in some of its portions like the "*Pārāyaṇavagga*" is that one should know the real nature of the world and having known it, should lead a moral life shaking off all philosophical views (*diṭṭhis*).

Similarly, a householder also must abide by some moral rules, because his occupation does not facilitate him to lead a perfectly spotless holy life. He must not harm or kill any living being, must not speak falsehood or steal things or to take intoxicating drinks. He should practise charity, honorable trade by right means and should dutifully maintain his parents.

The *Sutta-Nipāta* stands unique in many respects:

(i) It emphasizes the historicity of the Buddha Gautama. It is free from all miraculous elements associated with the biography of the Buddha, which we come across in the canonical books.

---

50. *Ibid.*

51. *Ibid.*, p. 237.

52. *Ibid.*, p. 235.

(ii) The portions of *Sutta-Nipāta* are primarily addressed to a monk because most of the *sutta*s preach the avoidance of all clinging.

(iii) In the *Sutta-Nipāta* "nuns" are not mentioned. It is evident by this fact that this book is related to the earliest part of the Pāli canon.

(iv) In this work the word "Buddha" is employed in such a way that it can be applied to any monk who attains the perfect enlightenment.

(v) According to Fausboll[53] in the *Sutta-Nipāta*, "sin" can be understood in two aspects. Subjectively it is understood as "desire" in various forms such as desire for existence, name and form, etc. Objectively "sin" lies in embodiment. Similarly, in this work[54] "Bliss" has also two aspects. Subjectively it is emancipation from desire by means of attaining peace. Objectively it is emancipation from body and matter. For instance, it is taught that those who have destroyed the seeds of existence go out like a "lamp." When one blows the flame it just goes out without leaving any trace. Likewise, a monk who is delivered from name and form disappears and cannot be characterised.

In the *Sutta-Nipāta*, we have an ambivalent teaching of *nirvāṇa*. Carefully viewed, we find six versions of *nirvāṇa* as referred to in different passages of the text.[55]

(i) *Nirvāṇa* as absolute annihilation of attachment, hatred and ignorance.

---

53. V. Fausboll (tr.), Introduction, pp. xv-xvi.

54. *Ibid.*, p. xvi.

55. V.V.S. Saibaba, *Nirvāṇa as Described in Sutta-Nipāta*, World Buddhism, vol. xxiv, no. 11, pp. 291-92.

(ii) *Anupādhisesha* or *parinirvāṇa* (freedom from aggregates).

(iii) Empirical view of *nirvāṇa* as realising the middle path by moderate living and avoiding the extremes which resembles the liberation taught by philosophers, like Epicures and Democritus.

(iv) Positivistic conception of *nirvāṇa* which supports the view that Buddhism is World-affirmating religion.

(v) Ethical conception of *nirvāṇa* described as complete abandonment of attachment, hatred and delusion, impurities, afflictions and the desire for existence.

(vi) Metaphysical conception of *nirvāṇa* described as the ineffable, non-mundane state which transcends all categorization and conceptualization.

Critically viewed the *Sutta-Nipāta* contributes to certain important ideas, which shaped Mahāyāna Buddhism later. For instance *Akiñchanatva* and *Śūnya* have become philosophical key words in later Buddhism. Similarly, notions like "nothingness," which occupies an important place in Mahāyāna Buddhism, are found in the *Sutta-Nipāta* in an embryonic stage. There are also some *suttas*, which hint the basic ideas of the Mādhyamika school of Mahāyāna Buddhism.

Uraga Vagga : Rhinoceros Sutta (Khaggavisāṇa Sutta)

The first Vagga of the *Sutta-Nipāta* was so named based on the *Uraga Sutta* of the first cantoe.[56] From the chronological point of view the *Khaggavisāṇa Sutta* is one of the earliest portions of the *Khuddhaka Nikāya*.[57] As regards its antiquity since the *Khaggavisāṇa Sutta* of the *Uragavagga* has been quoted

---

56. O Abeynayake, *op. cit.*, p. 134.

57. *Ibid.*, p. 77.

in the *Vinaya*, the *Saṁyutta* and the *Aṅguttara Nikāyas* of the Pāli canon and in view of the latter's precedence to "*Niddesa*" its canonical commentary it is regarded as one of the earliest elements of the *Sutta-Nipāta*.[58]

The *gāthās* of the *Khadgavisāṇa Sutta* are probably earlier than those of the corresponding *Khaggavisāṇa Sutta* in the Pāli *Sutta-Nipāta*.[59] The *Khaggavisāṇa Sutta* is inserted in the *Paccekabuddhapadāna* of the *Apadāna*, another independent treatise of the *Khuddaka Nikāya* which deals with the glorification of the *Paccekabuddhas*.[60] The *Khaggavisāṇa Sutta* presents the *Udānas* preached by the *Paccekabuddhas*.[61] In forty-one vigorous stanzas this Sutta depicts the significance of the solitary life of the Buddhist monk with an earnestness and pathos. The *Culla-Niddesa* (Short Explanation) explains the *Khaggavisāṇa Sutta* of the *Uragavagga*.

The *Rhinoceros Sutta* is one of the best examples that can be taken by those who claim Buddhism as world-negating religion. The "rhinoceros" is a metaphor meant for just as in Christianity sheep and shepherd are metaphors that indicate a disciple and prophet guide. The *Rhinoceros Sutta* explains through several similes that family life and intercourse with others should be avoided, for society has all vices in its train. Therefore, one should leave the corrupted state of society and lead a solitary life.

Animal "rhinoceros," which wanders in solitude, symbolizes a solitary mendicant who strives towards the goal of *nirvāṇa*. The Buddha teaches that an ascetic should abandon

---

58. Lord Chalmers, *op. cit.*, Introduction, p. xviii.
59. M. Winternitz, *op. cit.*, p. 247.
60. *Ibid.*, p. 158.
61. O Abeynayake, *op. cit.*, p. 125.

a fixed abode and all relations by avoiding all ties. Just like a shoot of a bamboo tree he should not cling to any thing. A wise ascetic should cut off all attachments and should just remain alone similar to a Kovilara tree that sheds all the leaves. Knowing that several pleasures are nothing but calamities, boils, misfortunes, diseases and dangers, overcoming all climatic disturbances like cold and heat freed from the fears of hunger, thirst and poisonous wild creatures, an ascetic would lead a free and independent life like a large elephant that roams freely in solitude. An ascetic who exerts for liberation should abandon all passions such as covetousness, deceit, craving, etc. He should seek a magnanimous righteous and wise friend, who upholds *dharma*:

> If one acquires a clever companion, an associate righteous and wise, let him, overcoming all dangers wander about with him glad and thoughtful.[62]
>
> Let one cultivate (the society of) a friend who is learned and keeps the *dhamma*, who is magnanimous and wise; knowing the meaning (of things) and subduing his doubts, let one wander alone like a rhinoceros.[63]

A true ascetic is advised to renunciate relations of all kinds such as parents, son, wife, etc. and material possessions such as wealth, corn, etc. acknowledging worldly pleasures as fishhooks.

> Having left son and wife, father and mother, wealth, and corn, and relatives, the different objects of desire, let one wander alone like a rhinoceros.[64]

---

62. *Sutta-Nipāta*, 44; V. Fausboll, *op. cit.*, p. 7.
63. *Sutta-Nipāta*, 57; V. Fausboll, *op. cit.*, p. 9.
64. *Sutta-Nipāta*, 59; V. Fausboll, *op. cit.*, p. 9.

> This is a tie, in this there is little happiness, little enjoyment, but more of pain, this is a "fish-hook," so having understood, let a thoughtful man wander alone like a rhinoceros.[65]

A follower of the Tathāgatha throwing out all fetters, being indifferent to pleasure and pain having acquired equanimity, tranquility and purity treads on the path of *nirvāṇa*. Endowed with psychophysical vitality, being energetic coupled with meditation an ascetic endeavours towards liberation. Just like a lion who does not tremble at noises like a wind not caught in a net, like a lotus not stained by water, like a fire which does not retreat to its burnt place, an ascetic wanders freely and independently being unconditioned and detached from everything.

> Having torn the ties, having broken the net as a fish in the water, being like a fire not returning to the burnt place, let one wander alone like a rhinoceros.[66]

> Like a lion not trembling at noises, like the wind not caught in a net, like lotus not stained by water, let one wander alone like a rhinoceros.[67]

The *Khaggavisāṇa Sutta* of *Uragavagga* exemplifies through striking metaphors, that the ties of a family life, vices and social life, material possessions, natural calamities and climatic disturbances cause pain or suffering by creating the fettered mind. In a society individuals are impure as they serve others with selfish motives. Hence a mendicant, overcoming all the philosophical views, cultivating kindness, equanimity, compassion, etc. wanders like the animal rhinoceros freely and independently. Thus, the *sutta* illustrates well that Buddhism is a religion of solitude and aloofness from all worldly

---

65. *Sutta-Nipāta*, 60; V. Fausboll, *op. cit.*, p. 9.
66. *Sutta-Nipāta*, 61; V. Fausboll, *op. cit.*, p. 9.
67. *Sutta-Nipāta*, 70; V. Fausboll, *op. cit.*, p. 11.

activities. When compared to Mahāyāna Buddhism the usual characteristic of rigorous and pessimistic attitude of Theravāda perspective of a monk or a mendicant is portrayed in the *Khaggavisāṇa Sutta.*

Book of the Octades (Aṭṭhakavagga)

According to B.C. Law,[68] the *Aṭṭhakavagga* of the *Sutta-Nipāta* appears as a separate work in other parts of the Pāli canonical works,[69] viz. the *Vinaya Piṭaka,* the *Saṁyutta Nikāya* and the *Udāna.* Despite the meaning of the title of the fourth cantoe of the *Sutta-Nipāta* being controversial, it is perhaps named "*Aṭṭhaka*" due to the inclusion of the four *Aṭṭhaka Sutta*s in this Vagga.[70] The *Mahā-Niddesa* (The Great Explanation) consists of the Commentary on the *Aṭṭhakavagga.*[71]

The *Aṭṭhakavagga* is the book of octos wherein two themes are prominently mentioned. This section firstly contains the teachings, which inculcates the ascetic virtues such as homelessness, refraining from all kinds of passion and avoiding all kinds of abundance. Secondly in eight *sutta*s of this section, it is taught that theoretic formulation of all sorts, philosophy, disputations and debates are stated as harmful to spiritual life. In *sutta*s of book-IV, various metaphors are intended to drive our attention to the point of the urgency of getting rid of desire and attachment to all possessions, material as well as psychological. According to the first *sutta,* viz. *Kāma Sutta* the avoidance of sensual pleasures is compared to the avoidance of treading upon the head of the snake.

---

68. B.C. Law, *op. cit.,* p. 233.
69. *Ibid.*
70. O. Abeynayake, *op. cit.,* pp. 134-35.
71. M. Winternitz, *op. cit.,* p. 156.

> He who avoids sensual pleasures as (he would avoid treading upon) the head of the snake with his foot, such a one, being thoughtful (*sato*), will conquer this desire.[72]

According to the second *sutta, Guhaṭṭhaka Sutta* unless one throws all attachments the ignorant people are deluded and tremble in selfishness, which may be compared to a fish in a dried-up stream.

> Look upon those men trembling in selfishness like fish in a stream nearly dried up, with little water. Seeing this let one wander about unselfish, without forming any attachment to existences.[73]

According to the third *sutta, Duṭṭhaṭṭhaka Sutta* the Buddhist monk should overcome all *dharma*s and *dogma*s of all philosophy. As the Buddha exhorts:

> But he who is dependent undergoes censure amongst the *dharmas*; With what (name) and how should one name him who is independent? For by him there is nothing grasped or rejected, he has in this world shaken off every (philosophical) view.[74]

According to the fourth *sutta, Suddhaṭṭhaka Sutta* due to a multi number of philosophical views a spiritual aspirant runs from one teacher to another endlessly just as a restless monkey jumps from one branch of a tree to another. No philosophical view can purify the mind of the person and lead a person to get rid off suffering completely. The only way for obtaining the purification of mind is the practice of noble eight-fold path which leads to the goal of *nirvāṇa*. A true Brāhmaṇa is one whose mind is freed from all attachments and who overcomes all dualities, which does not cling to good and evil is qualified

---

72. *Sutta-Nipāta*, 768; V. Fausboll, *op. cit.*, p. 146.
73. *Sutta-Nipāta*, 777; V. Fausboll, *op. cit.*, p. 147.
74. *Sutta-Nipāta*, 787; V. Fausboll, *op. cit.*, p. 150.

for attaining the goal of *nirvāṇa*. The word "Brāhmaṇa" is not used as a racial term here. The Buddha defines a true Brāhmaṇa as follows:

> But the Brāhmaṇa who does not cling to what has been seen, or heard, to virtue and (holy) works, or to what has been thought, to what is good and to what is evil, and who leaves behind what has been grasped, without doing anything in this world, he does not acknowledge that purification comes from another.[75]

According to the fifth *sutta*, *Paramaṭṭhaka-Sutta* it is stated that the people who boast of their learning wish to debate between different views. The Buddha rejects all philosophical views based on the knowledge of virtue and holy works. The mind of a Buddhist monk will not be impressed by any *dharma* as he gives up all desires.

> They do not form (any views), they do not prefer (anything), The *dhammas* are not chosen by them; a brāhmaṇa is not dependent upon virtue and (holy) works; having gone to the other shore, such a one does not return.[76]

According to the sixth *sutta*, viz. *Garā Sutta* the Buddha taught that selfishness, avarice are accompanied by grief, which result in disappointment and dismay. Life is so short that the living person disappears before us passing away like a dream object. Hence a *bhikṣu* does not cling to what is seen, heard and thought just as water does not stick to a lotus leaf such a *bhikṣu* will be free from the reiterated existence.

> For a *bhikkhu*, who wanders about unattached and cultivates the mind of a recluse, they say it is proper that he does not show himself (again) in existence.[77]

---

75. *Sutta-Nipāta*, 790; V. Fausboll, *op. cit.*, p. 151.

76. *Sutta-Nipāta*, 803; V. Fausboll, *op. cit.*, p. 154.

77. *Sutta-Nipāta*, 810; V. Fausboll, *op. cit.*, p. 155.

According to the seventh *sutta,* viz. *Tissametteya Sutta,* the fundamental teaching is that sexual intercourse should be abandoned. Whoever transcends all kinds of sensory attachments attains *nirvāṇa.*

> Designated "wise" he has entered upon a solitary life, then having given himself up to sexual intercourse, he (being) a fool suffers pain.[78]

The eighth *sutta,* viz., *Pasūra Sutta* emphasizes the futility of arguments and debates. Ratiocination will not give us any glimpse of truth. The disputant ignorantly thinks depending on the single truths that their respective doctrines only contain purity. But an expert would say that purification takes place in dispute because the field of exaltation will also be one's defeat. Attachment to any particular doctrine is condemned by the Buddha including the intra-Buddhist disputes:

> Those who wander about after having secluded themselves, without opposing view to view — what (opposition) wilt thou meet with amongst those, O Pasura, by whom nothing in this world is grasped as the best.[79]

The ninth *sutta,* viz. *Māgandiya Sutta* contains a dialogue between a brāhmaṇa known as Māgandiya and the Buddha. The Buddha while rejecting the former's offer of his daughters in marriage says that he has conquered *Taṇhā, Rati* and *Rāga*, the three daughters of the Māra. Marriage life is not the ingredient of the good life. When brāhmaṇa Māgandiya argues that purity comes from philosophy the Buddha explains that neither grasping of any view, tradition, knowledge, virtue, and holy works nor by the absence of the above one obtains purity.

---

78. *Sutta-Nipāta*, 820; V. Fausboll, *op. cit.*, p. 157.

79. *Sutta-Nipāta*, 833; V. Fausboll, *op. cit.*, p. 159.

> An accomplished man does not by (a philosophical) view, or by thinking become arrogant, for he is not of that sort; not by (holy) works, nor by tradition is he to be led, he is not led into any of the resting places (of the mind).[80]

In other words, the Buddha teaches that there should be no ideology and commitment. Elucidating this, the Buddha exhorts:

> For him who is free from marks there are no ties, to him who is delivered by understanding there are no follies (but those) that grasped after marks and (philosophical) views, they wander about in the world annoying (people).[81]

According to the tenth *sutta, Purābheda Sutta* a *muni* is one who has restraint in his speech, who is detached, not deceitful, etc. A calm *muni* is he, who overcomes desire, who has no ties, material possessions such as cattle, field, etc. who grasps nothing and rejects nothing. Similar to the *Khaggavisāṇa Sutta* of the *Uragavagga "Purābheda Sutta"* also represents Buddhism as world-negating religion

> Free from covetousness, without avarice, the *muni* does not reckon himself amongst the distinguished, nor amongst the plain, nor amongst the low, he does not enter time, being delivered from time.[82]

According to eleventh *sutta,* viz. *Kalahavivāda Sutta,* the Buddha explains the interconnected fabric of the dependent origination and points out the dependence of all human activity on grasping name and form, consciousness, etc.

> And having known these to be dependent the investigating *muni,* having known the things we depend upon, and after

---

80. *Sutta-Nipāta,* 846; V. Fausboll, *op. cit.,* p. 162.

81. *Sutta-Nipāta,* 847; V. Fausboll, *op. cit.,* p. 162.

82. *Sutta-Nipāta,* 860; V. Fausboll, *op. cit.,* p. 164.

> knowing them being liberated, does not enter into dispute, the wise (man) does not go to reiterated existence.[83]

The theme of the twelfth *sutta*, viz. *Kūlaviyūha Sutta* is as follows: Various philosophers advocate their own theories as the only truth and what is claimed by their opponents is not so. Why do even those who claim to be wise and expert maintain contradictory views? And why do they brand each other as fools? The Śramaṇas and Tīrthaṅkaras have the tendency to assert the contradictory truths and dispute each other. But the Buddha teaches that "the truth is one" without a second. There are not many different truths in the world. Except consciousness there is no eternal truth.

> For the truth is one, there is not a second, about which one intelligent man might dispute with another intelligent man; (but) they themselves praised different truths, therefore the Samanas do not say one (and the same thing).[84]

According to the thirteenth *sutta*, viz. *Mahāviyuha Sutta* by means of advocating philosophical views or organizing debates one cannot obtain contentment and attains tranquility.

> Having abandoned his former passions, not contracting new ones, not wandering according to his wishes, being no dogmatist, he is delivered from the (philosophical) views, being wise and he does not cling to the world, neither does he blame himself.[85]

However, one cultivates virtue and performs holy works, one still feels discontentment thinking that he has not acquired enough virtue and performed all the holy works which are expected to be necessary for attaining liberation. Even in the

---

83. *Sutta-Nipāta*, 877; V. Fausboll, *op. cit.*, p. 167.
84. *Sutta-Nipāta*, 884; V. Fausboll, *op. cit.*, p. 168.
85. *Sutta-Nipāta*, 913; V. Fausboll, *op. cit.*, p. 174.

desire to be pure as well as in the reckless immoral life the craving for existence is not absent. In other words, dogmatism, righteousness described by non-Buddhists or indifference to ethics and indulgence in sense-enjoyment none of these will lead us to the goal of *nirvāṇa*. A true brāhmaṇa is one who is independent, passionless and is liberated from "time."

> Being secluded amongst all the doctrines (*dhamma*), whatever has been seen, heard, or thought, he is a *muni* who has laid down his burden and is liberated, not belonging to time (*na kappiyo*), not dead, not wishing for anything. So said Bhāgavat.[86]

According to the teaching of the fourteenth *sutta*, viz. *Tuvaṭaka Sutta* a wise *bhikṣu* should annihilate the multiplicity of name and form (*nāmarūpa*) based on *avidya*. Such a *bhikkhu* has inward appeasement.

> Let the *bhikkhu* be appeased inwardly, let him not seek peace from any other (quarter); for him who is inwardly appeased there is nothing grasped or rejected.[87]

His mind is stilled like ocean's depth, which is waveless. A *bhikṣu* should cultivate discipline by restricting himself to the necessities of life. He should not resort to activities like cheating, *mantra*s, interpreting dream signs, stars, the cries of the birds, etc. The Buddha also lays down the rules of general guidance for a *bhikṣu*'s behaviour such as that a monk should not store any foodstuffs and clothes. He should not sleep too much. He should not participate in the sports; and should not indulge in sexual intercourse.

According to the teaching of the fifteenth *sutta*, *Attadaṇḍa Sutta* a monk who adheres to the Buddha *dharma* should

---

86. *Sutta-Nipāta*, 914; V. Fausboll, *op. cit.*, p. 174.

87. *Sutta-Nipāta*, 919; V. Fausboll, *op. cit.*, p. 175.

cultivate desirelessness by acknowledging that desire is precipitation, craving, a bog of lust which is difficult to cross.

> For him who is free from desire, for the discerning (man) there is no *samkhāra*; abstaining from every sort of effort he sees happiness everywhere.[88]

An accomplished monk will set aside what is before, middle and beyond. He considers himself neither low nor equal nor distinguished to others.

> What is before (thee), lay that aside; let there be nothing behind thee, if thou wilt not grasp after what is in the middle, thou will, wander calm.[89]

According to the teaching of the sixteenth *sutta*; *Śāriputta-Sutta* in the dialogue between venerable Sāriputra and the Buddha, the latter explains the kind of life a *bhikṣu* should lead. A wise *bhikṣu* should not be afraid of the five dangers namely, mosquitos gadflies, snakes, evil men, and quadrupeds. Having guided by wisdom he should overcome all the climatic disturbances, etc., The *bhikṣu* should overcome the four causes of lamentation. He abandons the five impurities of the world, having acquired equanimity and becomes liberated.

> Let him be with down-cast eyes, and not prying, devoted to meditation, very watchful; having acquired equanimity let him with a composed mind cut off the seat of doubt, and misbehaviour.[90]

Book of the Way-Across (Pārāyaṇa Vagga)

The title *Pārāyaṇa* of the fifth cantoe of the *Sutta-Nipāta* is so named as the *sutta*s of this cantoe deal with how to attain the

---

88. *Sutta-Nipāta*, 953; V. Fausboll, *op. cit.*, pp. 179-80.
89. *Sutta-Nipāta*, 949; V. Fausboll, *op. cit.*, p. 179.
90. *Sutta-Nipāta*, 972; V. Fausboll, *op. cit.*, p. 182.

goal of *nibbāna* by crossing over the ocean of *saṁsāra*. Lord Chalmers asserts[91] that whereas the text consists of independent and unconnected poems, the *Pārāyaṇavagga* aims at a dramatic synthesis and among the five cantoes, the fifth, i.e., *Pārāyaṇavagga* is unique owing to its purposeful unity.[92]

The *Pārāyaṇavagga* is reffered to six times as a separate poem in the Nikāyas.[93] It is mentioned in the *Saṁyutta*, *Aṅguttara Nikāya*s of the Pāli canon and in the Chinese *Tripiṭaka*.[94] We come across the *Aṅguttara Nikāya*, verses quoted from the text *Pārāyaṇa* and not from the *Sutta-Nipāta* wherein we find the word *Pārāyaṇa*.[95] In the fifth cantoe sixteen *sutta*s are strung together by the framework of a story. It is evident that *Pārāyaṇavagga* has once existed as a separate poem. It is so treated by the commentator who calls it a *suttānta*.[96] The *Pārāyaṇavagga* had undergone some minor changes when it was incorporated in the *Sutta-Nipāta*.

The non-mention of the river Godāvarī in the earlier text proves the later origin of the *Vatthu Gāthā*s of the *Pārāyaṇa-vagga*.[97] The non-existence of the *Vatthu Gāthā*s of the *Pārāyaṇa-vagga* in the *Niddesa* underlies the fact that the present version of the *Sutta-Nipāta* including those *Vatthu Gāthā*s was compiled later than the *Niddesa*. It is evident from the absence of the *Vatthu Gāthā* in the *Niddesa* that they were not connected to the main text. Most probably the compiler of the *Sutta-Nipāta*

---

91. Lord Chalmers, *op. cit.*, Introduction, p. xiii.
92. *Ibid.*
93. B.C. Law, *op. cit.*, p. 234; O. Abeynayake, *op. cit.*, p. 76.
94. *Ibid.*, p. 75, fns. 2,9.
95. See *Aṅguttara Nikāya*, III. 32; M. Winternitz, *op. cit.*, p. 69, fn. 2.
96. O. Abeynayake, *op. cit.*, p. 75.
97. *Ibid.*, pp. 77-78.

had added the *Vatthu Gāthās* as the epilogue to the *Pārāyaṇa-vagga*.[98]

At the age of the first four Pāli Nikāyas the sixteen sections of the *Pārāyaṇavagga* were entitled as *Pañha*. For instance we find expressions like *Pārāyaṇa Punnakapañha*, *Pārāyaṇo Udayapañha* and *Pārāyaṇe Metteyya Pañha*.[99] In the early canonical texts like the *Aṅguttara Nikāya* the poems were named as *Pañha*. Later at the time of the composition of the *Sutta-Nipāta* they were called as *Pucchā*. At the time of Pāli commentaries they were included in the group of *suttas*. That is why the commentator calls them as *Sutta* instead of *Pucchā*.

The Book of the Way-Across narrates a story of a brāhmaṇa Bāvarī who was well versed in the Vedic lore. He went from the city of Kośala to south (*dakṣiṇa pāṭha*) in pursuit of Nothingness (*akiñcanna*). He dwelt on the banks of Godāvarī living on fruits, etc. in the neighbourhood of Alakā in Emperor Aśoka's territory. He performed a great sacrifice with the aid of the people of the village. Having completed it, while re-entering his hermitage, he was asked by an ugly brāhmaṇa a sum of five hundred rupees in charity. When Bāvarī replied that he spent all the money in the performance of sacrifice, he received a curse of death by the ugly brāhmaṇa who said, "May thy head on the seventh day hence cleave into seven." When Bāvarī became sorrowful struck with grief, the benevolent deity of that place comforted him by telling that the brāhmaṇa who cursed him was a hypocrite, the deity also referred the Buddha as an enlightened one and provided the necessary information of his dwelling place. Then Bāvarī sent his sixteen learned disciples such as Ajita, Tissametteya, and Punnaka, etc. to enable them know the *dharma* or the highest

98. *Ibid.*, p. 136.

99. *Ibid.*, pp. 136-37.

truth. Bāvarī told his sixteen disciples how to recognise the Buddha by his thirty-two holy marks of a perfect man and if they have questions in their minds about Bāvarī's birth, family, marks, hymns and disciples, if he is a true Buddha he would answer them.

Having travelled a long way from south India through cities like Alakā, Māhissatī, Uggeni, Gonaddha, Vedisā, Vanasavhaya, Kośambī, Sāketa, Sāvatthi, Setavya, Kapilavastu, Kusināra, Pāva, the city of wealth and Vesālī the city of Magadha, they reached the Pāsānaka the Rock temple, where they found Bhagavan Buddha preaching the *dharma* in the assembly of *bhikkhus*. After observing the marks of perfection on the limbs of the Buddha, Agita, one of Bāvarī's disciples, asked in his mind the question of his master's birth, marks, family, perfection in hymns, etc. The enlightened one responded that Bāvarī was one hundred-twenty years old, he was Bāvarī by family, there were three marks of perfection on his limbs, he was perfect in three Vedas, his master could recite five hundred hymns and attained perfection in his own *dharma*. After hearing their master's marks of perfection and other details Agita requested the Buddha to clear his doubts regarding the meaning of head and head splitting. The Buddha replied that ignorance is the head, which is cleaved by the knowledge together with belief, thoughtfulness, meditation, determination and strength. Acknowledging the Buddha's omniscience, the sixteen disciples of the Buddha enquired about their doubts.

(i) *Agitamāṇava Pucchā*: In reply to enquiries made by Ajita, Buddha taught that ignorance shrouds the world. Because of avarice, it does not shine. Desire pollutes it. Thoughtfulness is the dam of the stream of desire and hence by the former is the latter stopped. By the cessation of consciousness name and form are totally stopped. The *bhikṣu* should not crave for sexual pleasures, shall cultivate calmness of mind and skill in *dharma*

> Buddha: Let the *bhikkhu* not crave for sensual pleasures, let him be calm in mind, let him wander about skilful in all *dhammas*, and thoughtful.[100]

(ii) *Tissametteyamāṇava Pucchā*: In reply to enquiries made by Tissametteya, Buddha spoke out that a *bhikṣu* who has abstained from sensuous pleasures, who are free from desires, who are thoughtful and happy by reflection is cut out and without commotion. Such a *bhikṣu* having known both ends do not stick in the middle as far as understanding is concerned and such a man is called great.

> The *bhikkhu* who abstains from sensual pleasures, — O Metteyya, so said Bhāgavat, — who is free from desire, always thoughtful, happy by reflection, he is without commotions, he after knowing both ends does not stick in the middle, as far as his understanding is concerned, him I call a great man. . . .[101]

(iii) *Puṇṇakamāṇava Pucchā*: In response to the question of venerable Puṇṇaka, the Buddha told that all sages, khattiyas and brāhmaṇas as a result of offering sacrifices to gods with a wish such as praise and sensual pleasures obtained something good here and hereafter. But they cannot transcend birth and old age. Those who are devoted to offering of sacrifices are subjected to passions of existence and do not transcend the cycle

---

100. *Sutta-Nipāta*, 1039; V. Fausboll, *op. cit.*, p. 191.

101. *Sutta-Nipāta*, 1041; V. Fausboll, *op. cit.*, p. 192.

of reiterated existence. Such transcendence is possible for him who is calm, without passions and is free from woe and desire.

> . . . he who is not defeated anywhere in the world, who is calm without the smoke of passions, free from woe, free from desire, he crosses over birth and old age. . . .[102]

(iv) *Mettagūmāṇava Pucchā*: In reply to Mettagū regarding the origin of pain and how does wise cross the stream of transmigration, the Buddha taught that suffering arises from aggregates (*upādhi*), while one created by ignorance. Therefore, the wise do not create *upādhi* and understand the truth of suffering without traditional instructions. One who lives thoughtful and strenuous possesses nothing and clings to nothing and longs for nothing crosses over the stream of birth and old age.

> Living so, thoughtful, strenuous, let the *bhikkhu* wandering about, after abandoning selfishness, birth, and old age and sorrow, and lamentation, being a wise man, leave pain in this world.[103]

(v) *Dhotakamāṇava Pucchā*: Asked by Dhotaka as to how one could learn his own extinction the Buddha exhorts that by exertion combined with wisdom and thoughtfulness, after listening to Buddha's words, one works out one's own *nirvāṇa*. Whoever overcomes desire in the world, does not thirst for reiterated existence, knows that everything around him is a tie across the stream of existence.

---

102. *Sutta-Nipāta*, 1047; V. Fausboll, *op. cit.*, p. 193.

103. *Sutta-Nipāta*, 1055; V. Fausboll, *op. cit.*, pp. 194-95.

> Whatsoever thou knows, — O Dhotaka, "so said Bhāgavat," (of what is) above, below, across, and in the middle, knowing this to be a tie in the world, thou must not thirst for reiterated existence.[104]

(vi) *Upasīvamāṇava Pucchā*: Asked by Upasīva as to the means by which one attains the goal of *nibbāna*, the Buddha replied that in crossing across the great stream, the one support, which one can have, is the discernment of nothingness of things. He who resorts to nothingness and is delivered by highest knowledge will never fall away. To the enquiry if that is the case, for a long time after he becomes tranquil and delivered will he have personality or consciousness, the answer is just as blown out flame by the wind cannot be reckoned or cognised even similarly a liberated *muni* disappears from the range of our cognition.

> As a flame blown about by the violence of the wind O Upasīva, so said Bhāgavat — goes out, cannot be reckoned (as existing), even so a *muni* delivered from name and body, disappears and cannot be reckoned(as existing).[105]

To the further enquiry of Upasīva, if the sage so disappears, does he cease to be? Or does he exist for ever free from sickness, the Buddha elucidates that of him who so disappears there is "no form or measure" because nothing can be said that he is or he is not, when all the *dharma*s have gone, all dispute and denoting terms come to an end.

> For him who has disappeared there is no form, O Upasīva, so said Bhāgavat. — That by which they say he is, exists for

---

104. *Sutta-Nipāta*, 1067; V. Fausboll, *op. cit.*, p. 197.

105. *Sutta-Nipāta*, 1073; V. Fausboll, *op. cit.*, p. 198.

> him no longer, when all things (*dhamma*) have been cut off, all (kinds of) disputes are also cut off.[106]

(vii) *Nandamāṇava Pucchā*: To the question by venerable Nanda as regards the definition of *muni*, the Buddha taught that one is called a *muni* in this world, not because he has any philosophical view, tradition or knowledge (*dṛṣṭi, śruti* and *jñāna*) but because he wanders freely from woe and desire after secluding himself. The śramaṇas and brāhmaṇas who say that purity comes from views, tradition, virtue and religious works, etc. do not transcend birth and old age. But those who leave what has been seen heard or thought including virtue and religious works transcend birth and old age.

> Buddha: Not because of (any philosophical view, nor of tradition, nor of knowledge), O Nanda, do the expert call (any one) a *muni*, (but) such as wander free from woe, free from desire, after having secluded themselves, those I call *munis*.[107]

(viii) *Hemakamāṇava Pucchā*: Upon the enquiry of venerable Hemaka about the *dhamma* which destroys craving, the Buddha told that the ending of passion as well of the desire, i.e., holding the objects to be clean is the state of *nibbāna* which is imperishable. To understand this is to see the tranquil and divine *dharma*.

> . . . the destruction of passion and of wish for the dear objects that have been perceived, O Hemaka, is the imperishable state of *nibbāna*.[108]

---

106. *Sutta-Nipāta*, 1075; V. Fausboll, *op. cit.*, p. 199.
107. *Sutta-Nipāta*, 1077; V. Fausboll, *op. cit.*, p. 199.
108. *Sutta-Nipāta*, 1085; V. Fausboll, *op. cit.*, p. 202.

(ix) *Todeyyamāṇava Pucchā*: In reply to the query of venerable Todeyya about the nature of deliverance of one who has no craving, the Buddha replied that Final release (*vimokkha*) is attained by him who has no craving and doubts. Such a man of deliverance longs for nothing and need not acquire any further understanding. Such a sage is possessed of understanding and knows the *dhamma*.

> He in whom there live no lusts, — O Todeyya, so said Bhāgavat, . . . to whom there is no desire, and who has overcome doubt, for him there is no other deliverance.[109]

(x) *Kappamāṇava Pucchā*: In response to the enquiry of venerable Kappa as to what is an island of those who suffer in this world and who overcome by decay and death, the Buddha taught that *nibbāna* is that matchless Island where there is no decay or death, where the old has passed away and the fresh does not find a place. Thus, the *muni* who is calm and thoughtful sees the *dhamma* not becoming the victim of Māra.

> This matchless island, possessing nothing (and) grasping after nothing, I call *nibbāna*, the destruction of decay and death.[110]

(xi) *Jatukaṇṇimāṇava Pucchā*: In pursuance of a request of venerable Jatukaṇṇī the Buddha instructed that wise should give up greed for sensuous pleasures, should forsake happiness in the world, should not grasp or reject anything in order to leave the world of decay and death and to reach the abode of peace.

---

109. *Sutta-Nipāta*, 1088; V. Fausboll, *op. cit.*, p. 202.

110. *Sutta-Nipāta*, 1093; V. Fausboll, *op. cit.*, p. 203.

> What is before thee, lay that aside; let there be nothing behind thee, if thou wilt not grasp after what is in the middle, thou wilt wander calm.[111]

(xii) *Bhadrāvudhamāṇava Pucchā*: To ven. Bhadrāvudha's enquiry on the nature of the liberated who is beyond time, the Buddha reiterated the importance of giving up all grasping and not to cling to anything. He warned those who grasp the phenomena around will be followed by Māra or fall into the power of death.

> Let one wholly subdue the desire of grasping (after everything), — O Bhadrāvudha, so said Bhāgavat, — above, below, across, and in the middle; for whatever they grasp after in the world, just by that Māra follows the man.[112]

(xiii) *Udayamāṇava Pucchā*: Replying to the queries of ven. Udaya about the deliverance by knowledge, the splitting up of ignorance, about the bond of the world and *nibbāna*, the nature of consciousness in a mindful sage, the Buddha enlightens the former by saying that ignorance is quenched by shedding appetite for joys and griefs and by quelling the grossness of the mind, with equanimity and thoughtfulness and reasoning on *dharma*, knowledge brings one to deliverance.

The world is bound by pleasure; thought explores the pleasures. Destruction of craving is *nirvāṇa*. For the sage who is mindful who does not delight in sexual pleasures both inwardly and outwardly individual consciousness ceases. The heritage of mind is dissipated.

---

111. *Sutta-Nipāta*, 1098; V. Fausboll, *op. cit.*, p. 204.

112. *Sutta-Nipāta*, 1102; V. Fausboll, *op. cit.*, p. 205.

> Buddha: The world is bound by pleasure, reasoning is its practice, by the leaving of desire *nibbāna* is said to be.[113]

(xiv) *Posālamāṇava Pucchā*: In his reply to venerable Posāla about the knowledge of perfectly accomplished one the Buddha told that the Tathāgata who knows all the phases of consciousness knows the delivered person as well as the stages attained by others. In other words only he who is completely delivered can know at what stage of deliverance or bondage any one is.

> Tathāgata, knowing all the faces of consciousness, — O Posāla, "so" said Bhāgavat, — knows (also) him who stands delivered, devoted to that (object).[114]

(xv) *Mogharājamāṇava Pucchā*: Having asked thrice by venerable Mogharājan how one should view this world holding which one escapes death, the Buddha advised him to look upon the world as void, and always being watchful after having destroyed the view of the self one can overcome death.

> Look upon the world as void, O Mogharājan, being always thoughtful; having destroyed the view of oneself (as really existing) so one may overcome death; the king of death will not see him who thus regards the world.[115]

(xvi) *Piṅgiyamāṇava Pucchā*: Requested by the old and feeble Piṅgiya to let him know how to overcome birth and decay the Buddha advised him that whoever is heedful,

---

113. *Sutta-Nipāta*, 1108; V. Fausboll, *op. cit.*, p. 206.

114. *Sutta-Nipāta*, 1113; V. Fausboll, *op. cit.*, p. 207.

115. *Sutta-Nipāta*, 1118; V. Fausboll, *op. cit.*, p. 208.

and diligently roots out craving, will be free from reiterated existence.

> . . . therefore thou, O Piṅgiya, shalt be heedful, and leave desire behind, that thou mayest never come to exist again.[116]

Thus, the sixteen disciples of Bāvarī got fitting and satisfactory replies to their queries from the Buddha. All the sixteen brāhmaṇas having understood the meaning and tenor of each question lived according to the *dhamma* and consequently were liberated. After returning from Pāsānaka *cetiya* at Magadha, when old Piṅgiya was relating Buddha's virtues to his master Bāvarī, the Buddha finding the maturity of knowledge shed his grace on both by his presence. The Buddha taught[117] that Faith (*śraddha*) saved a number of notables such as Vakkali, Bhadrāvudha and Āḷavi Gautama in the past and if they also allow faith to save them they will also pass beyond the unending cycle of transmigration.

---

116. *Sutta-Nipāta*, 1122; V. Fausboll, *op. cit.*, p. 209.

117. V. Fausboll, *op. cit.*, p. 213.

6

Mahāyāna Buddhist Classics

VAJRACCHEDIKĀ PRAJÑĀPĀRAMITĀ

Introduction

The Prajñāpāramitā literature is the most ancient, authentic and sacred literature in Mahāyāna Buddhism. It deals with "Perfection of Wisdom" which constitutes the philosophical basis of Mahāyāna Buddhist thought.[1] The *Prajñāpāramitā Sūtras* are the earliest of Mahāyāna Sūtras which came into existence. Eminent Buddhist scholars differ in their opinion regarding the significant question when and where the composition of Prajñāpāramitā took place. Japanese scholars[2] viz. R. Yamada, K. Midzuno assert that the *Prajñāpāramitā Sūtra*s first came into existence in South India especially in Andhra among the Mahāsaṅghika Buddhist sect. Against this view scholars like E. Lammotte contend[3] that Mahāyāna came into existence in north-western and central India. The Prajñāpāramitā literature comprises different versions of *sūtra*s from largest to smallest besides several commentaries and sub-commentaries on them.

---

1. H. Nakamura, *Indian Buddhism*, p. 159.
2. *Ibid.*, p. 159, fn. 6.
3. *Ibid.*

There are several versions of Prajñāpāramitā[4] viz., the *Śatasāhasrikā*, the *Pañcaviṁśatisāhasrikā*, the *Aṣṭādaśasāhasrikā*, the *Daśasāhasrikā*, the *Sarddhadvisāhasrikā* or the *Suvikrāntavikrāmī-paripṛccha*, the *Buddha-Bhasita-Nīta-Artha-Prajñāpāramitā*, the *Aṣṭasāhasrikā*, the *Adhyardhaśatikā* or *Śatapañcasatikā*, the *Śaptaśatikā*, the *Pañcaṣatikā*, the *Vajracchedikā* or *Trimsatika*, the *Prajñāpāramitā Hṛdaya*, the *Kauśika Prajñāpāramitā*, the *Alpākṣarā* or *Svalpākṣarā*, and *Ekāksara Prajñāpāramitā* which are preserved in Sherphian section of Kanjur available in the form of twenty-one Tibetan translated works. Besides the above there are a number of *Prajñāpāramitā sūtras* which are found as extinct viz. the *Prajñāpāramitā-Ardhasatika*, the *Nagasripariprccha*, the *Devaraja-pravara-Prajñāpāramitā*, the *Karunika-rāja Prajñāpāramitā*, the *Pañcapāramitānirdesa*, the *Sūryagarbha*, and *Chandragarbha Prajñāpāramitā Mahāyāna Sūtras*, the *Samantabhadra Prajñāpāramitā*, the *Vajrapāṇi Prajñāpāramitā*, the *Vajraketu Prajñāpāramitā*, the *Aṣṭaśatikā*, the *Pañcavimśati-Prajñāpāramitā-Mukha*, and also several Dhāraṇis discovered in the Nepalese and Tibetan collections.

The *Vajracchedikā Prajñāpāramitā* is one of the Prajñāpāramitā literature comprising about thirty-eight[5] or forty[6] different *sūtras* composed in India between 100 BC - 600 CE. According to L.M. Joshi,[7] although it is difficult to decide the date of the *Vajracchedikā* we may certainly infer that it is composed after the *Aṣṭasāhasrikā* since, as E. Conze hinted, atleast in eight places the sentences and the glimpses of ideas of *Aṣṭasāhasrikā* can be

---

4. L.M. Joshi (ed. & tr.), *Vajracchedikā Prajñāpāramitā Sūtra with the commentary of Asaṅga*, p. 22; H. Nakamura, *op. cit.*, pp. 161-65; E. Conze, *The Prajñāpāramitā Literature*, pp. 37-87.

5. E. Conze (tr.), *The Diamond Sūtra and the Heart Sūtra in Buddhist Wisdom books*, see Preface.

6. L.M. Joshi, *op. cit.*, see Introduction, p. 1.

7. *Ibid.*, p. 3.

seen in the *Vajracchedikā*. It is quoted[8] twice in Śāntideva's *Sikṣāsamuccaya*, in Prajñākāramati's *Bodhicaryāvatāra Pañjikā*, in *Candrakīrti's Prasaññapada* and *Catuḥsataka Vṛtti* and in Haribhadra's *Abhisamayālaṅkāra-lokavyākhyā*. According to Hajime Nakamura[9] and L.M. Joshi,[10] the origin of the *Vajracchedikā* may be placed respectively between 150-200 CE and third or fourth *c.* CE. The antiquity of the *Vajracchedikā* may be inferred as very early from the fact that according to T. Shiomi, its teachings were exclusively delivered to only 1250 monks at Jetāvana[11] whose scheme according to H. Nakamura, was inherited by earliest *Mahāyāna Sūtras*[12] from the early *Buddhist Sūtras* which refer to Jetāvana or Veluvana as the venue of the Buddha's sermons and only 1250 *bhikṣus* without the presence of Bodhisattvas as the audience.

The *Vajracchedikā* which is originally written in Sanskrit is variously rendered into English as "Adamantine Perfection of Wisdom,"[13] "Diamond Cutter" or "Transcendent Wisdom"[14] or the "Sūtra of Wonderful effects."[15] It is so named[16] that it cuts or pierces the ignorance like a diamond or thunderbolt. But L.M. Joshi holds[17] that it is not proper to call it after some

---

8. *Ibid.*, p. 4.
9. H. Nakamura, *op. cit.*, p. 160, fn. 8.
10. L.M. Joshi, *op. cit.*, p. 3.
11. H. Nakamura, *op. cit.*, p. 160, fn. 10.
12. *Ibid.*, p. 159.
13. E. Conze (tr.) *The Diamond Sūtra and the Heart Sūtra in Buddhist Wisdom books*, p. 51.
14. F. Max Müller (tr.) The Vagrakkhedikā in Buddhist Mahāyāna Texts. part-2, see Introduction, p. xii.
15. *Ibid.*, see Introduction, p. xiii.
16. L.M. Joshi *op. cit.*, see Introduction, p. i.
17. *Ibid.*

Western scholars as Diamond Sūtra because in Buddhism *Prajñā* is like a diamond but is not meant in English as "diamond or thunderbolt." Here *vajra* is used in the esoteric sense which denotes *śūnyatā* or *prajñā* like a sword which cuts off one's defilements and ignorance in accordance with the Pāli *Abhidhamma* usage in *dhammasaṅganī*[18] and its commentary[19] wherein *prajñā* is called as the weapon which cuts the defilements. In Buddhist *tantras* also *prajñā* is called as *vajra* and Advayavajra had written a Vajrayāna commentary known as *Advayavajra Saṅgraha*. Edward Conze contends[20] that the simile of cutting or piercing is clearly indicated through the icons of Prajñāpāramitā and Mañjuśrī who are shown with swords. Hence the title of the treatise, i.e., *Vajracchedikā* is in accordance with its subject and content.

The *Vajracchedikā* is the ninth section of the long text entitled *Mahāprajñāpāramitā Sūtra*.[21] The *Prajñāpāramitā sūtras* in general and the *Vajracchedikā* in particular are regarded as the most precious and sacred canonical writings by the northern Mahāyāna Buddhists. The *Vajracchedikā* is one of the earliest and finest shorter *sūtras* most widely read and highly valued metaphysical treatises in Buddhist literature. It is a widely popular work[22] not only in China and Tibet but also in Middle Asia and Mongolia. The *Vajracchedikā* was very enthusiastically transmitted, recited, explained and commented upon[23] in Tibet, China and Japan. It is praised "as the holiest of the

---

18. *Ibid*., p. 2, fn.1; Bhikkhu J. Kashyap (ed.), *Dhammasaṅgani* p. 21.
19. See *Aṭṭhasālinī*, p. 148; L.M. Joshi, *op. cit.*, p. 2 fn. 2.
20. *Ibid*., see Introduction, p. 2.
21. H. Nakamura, *op. cit.*, p. 160.
22. E. Conze (tr.) *The Diamond Sūtra*, Introduction, p. iii.
23. H. Nakamura, *op. cit.*, p. 161 fn. 14.

holy"[24] by the Buddhists of thirty generations in China, Japan, Tibet and Mongolia. The popularity of this *sūtra* is far greater in Tibet, China and Japan than in India, the land of its origin.[25] The followers of the eighth century Ch'an had placed the *Vajracchedikā* above all other *sūtras*.[26] It is one of the two vastly studied Mahāyāna sūtras in Japan mainly by the followers of Shingon Buddhist sect,[27] the other being the *Prajñāpāramitā Hṛdaya*. The wide popularity of the *Vajracchedikā* in ancient times is evinced by its Tibetan, Khotanese, Sogdian, Mongolian and Munchurian translations and in modern times by its seven English, two French, two German, four Japanese, one Modern Japanese and a Hindi translation. Its authencity is evident from several commentaries and critical notes written by Indian and Chinese Buddhist scholars. According to Matsumoto[28] and Kogetsu,[29] many manuscript copies of original of the *Vajracchedikā* have been discovered in Central Asia. According to E. Leumann,[30] the fragments of the *sūtra* have also been found in the north Āryan language or Khotanese.

The following are the Sanskrit editions[31] of the *Vajracchedikā*:

(a) The Sanskrit text of the *Vajracchedikā* published by F. Max Müller.

(b) A revised new edition published by Edward Conze.

(c) The Central Asian text found by Sir Aurel Stein.

---

24. E.Conze (tr.) *The Diamond Sūtra*, see preface
25. H. Nakamura, *op. cit.*, p. 161.
26. E. Conze, *The Prajñāpāramitā Literature*, p. 31.
27. F. Max Müller, *op. cit.*, Introduction, p. xii.
28. H. Nakamura, *op. cit.*, p. 63, fn. 34.
29. *Ibid.*, pp. 160-61; p. 161, fn.11.
30. *Ibid.*, p. 161, fn. 12.
31. *Ibid.*, p. 160, fn. 9.

(d) The Gilgit text edited by N.P. Chakravarti.

(e) The Khotanese text found also by Sir Aurel Stein in Turfan.

Due to their close affinity with the indigenous neo-Taoist tradition in China Prajñāpāramitā translations had a significant influence on the progress of Buddhist thought. This is evident from the six Chinese translations of *Vajracchedikā* by scholars[32] namely Kumārajīva (402 CE), Bodhiruchi (509 CE), Paramārtha (562 CE), Dharmagupta (592 CE) Hiuen-tsang (660-663 CE) and I-tsing (703 CE). The *Vajracchedikā* was translated into Tibetan by Silendrabodhi and Ye-ses-sde. The Khotanese edition was done by Stenkonow; the Sogdian editions were prepared by H. Reichelt (1931) and F. Weller (1936). The Mongolian translation was secured by Baron Schiling de Canstadt and the Manchurian translation was prepared by M. De Harlez (1897). The Sanskrit text of *Vajracchedikā* was explained into Japanese by Bunyu Nanjio (1909). It was translated into Japanese by Sogen Yamagami (1917), by Shimizu Ryosho (1941), by H. Ui, by Gadjin Nagao (1973) and into modern Japanese by H. Nakamura and K. Kino (1961).

The *Vajracchedikā* was translated into French by Ch.de Harlez (1891) and a partial French translation from Tibetan by A. David-Neel (1958). There are two German translations by M. Schmidt (1837) and by M. Walleser (1914). The *Vajracchedikā* was translated into English by S. Beal (1864-65), F. Max Müller (1894), William Gemmel (1912; 1913), Waitao and D. Goddard (1935), A.F. Price (1947; 1955), D.T. Suzuki (1935; 1950, 1956, 1960) and Edward Conze (1958).

---

32. E. Conze, *The Prajñāpāramitā Literature*, p. 65; L.M. Joshi, *op. cit.*, Introduction, p. iii.

There are as many as 15 commentaries[33] including sub-commentaries on the *Vajracchedikā Prajñāpāramitā* in Sanskrit, Chinese and Tibetan. They are:

(1) Asaṅga's commentary entitled *Triśatikāyāḥ Prajñāpāramitāyāḥ Kārikāsaptati.*

  (a) Vasubandhu's sub-commentary on Asaṅga's commentary which was translated into Chinese by Bodhiruci (509 CE) and Yi-Ching (711 CE).

  (b) Vajrarsi's sub-commentary on Asaṅga's commentary which was translated into Chinese by Bodhiruci, K'uei-chi and I-tsing.

(2) The commentary was authored by Vasubandhu which is extinct whose Chinese translation is attributed to Dharmagupta (600 CE) and Tibtan translation is attributed to Dbyig Guen translated by Gshondpal (1450 CE)

(3) The commentary authored by Sridatta or Gunada which was rendered into Chinese by Divakara (683 CE).

(4) The commentary authored by Kamalaśīla which was rendered into Tibetan by Manjusri, Jinamitra and Ye-ses-sde.

The other nine Chinese commentaries on the *Vajracchedikā* are respectively attributed to (i) Chih-I, (ii) Chi-tsang, (iii) K'uei-chi, (iv) Tsung-mi, (v) Tzu-hsuan, (vi) Tsung-lei and Ju-ch', (vii) Chih-yen, (viii) Lu-tsu, and (ix) Han-shan.

Central Teachings

The *Vajracchedikā Prajñāpāramitā* is a short treatise which consists of 32 chapters. It comprises 300 *sloka*s and hence called by

33. E. Conze, *The Prajñāpāramitā Literature*, p. 67.

Acharya Asaṅga as *Trimśatikā Prajñāpāramitā*. According to Bunyiu Nanjio's catalogue of the *Tripiṭaka* the *Vajracchedikā* belongs to the ninth section of the *Mahā-prajñāpāramita-Sūtra* and it corresponds to the Tibetan translation of the text in 300 verses.[34] The ancient Tibetan scholars included the *Vajracchedikā* in the collection of 17 *sūtras* categorized as "*Matru-putra*."[35] The Sanskrit original of the *sūtra* does not mention any chapter division. The chapter division given in Kumārajīva's Chinese translation was adopted by Max Müller and subsequent scholars.

Vajracchedikā is in the form of a dialogue between ven. Subhūti and the Buddha. The central theme of *Vajracchedikā* is the teaching of *śūnyatā*. It appeals "directly to a spiritual intuition" which discards all logical conventions and enunciates the "doctrine of emptiness established in an ontological, psychological and logical form."[36] A.F. Price contends that *Vajracchedikā* can be understood as "the Discourse on the penetration of Impenetrable."[37] The *Vajracchedikā* adopts a peculiar style since a series of statements are made in repetitive ways in the *sūtra*. Therefore, in Max Müller's words[38] the *Vajracchedikā* represents a treatise on "metaphysical agnosticism" for it brings us into trans-conciousness, without producing any continuous sustained argument. Another significant feature of the *Vajracchedikā* is that in its attitudes and beliefs it differs from other religions. Edward Conze sums up the message of the *Vajracchedikā* in five central teachings[39]

34. F. Max Müller, *op. cit.*, Introduction, p. xiii.
35. L.M. Joshi, *op. cit.*, see Ven. Samdhong Rinpoche's statement
36. E. Conze, *The Prajñāpāramitā Literature*, p. 19.
37. A.F. Price (tr.), *The Diamond Sūtra* (trd. from Chinese) p. 42.
38. F. Max Müller, *op. cit.*, Introduction, p. xv.
39. Karl H. Potter (ed.) *Encyclopaedias of Indian Philosophies*, vol. VIII, p. 348.

viz. One should not (i) "perceive a self," a being, a living soul, or a person, (ii) "perceive a *dharma*," or separate entity, (iii) not establish one's thoughts anywhere, (iv) everything is not itself, and (v) The Buddha and his Enlightenment are transcendental.

The *Vajracchedikā* endeavors to teach us that all diverse objects which are based on their *dharma*, are illusive and subjective. They are the products of our own mind. The law of dependent origination governs all phenomena, which are produced by causes and conditions. As long as conditions exist things begin to appear and when conditions cease, things likewise cease to exist just as the foam of water, the lightning flash, vanishing clouds, etc. They are only momentary and have no essence of their own. Therefore, there is no truth in dualities like pure and impure, rough and fine, large and small, far and near and knowable and unknowable.

Whereas phenomena are divided into "perceptible and knowable" and "imperceptible and unknowable," through habitual delusions, boundless worlds, innumerable verities of things spring up in the mind. These subtle ideas are not perceptible and knowable except by those who seek enlightenment, i.e., Bodhisattvas. Although there are two forms of existence namely perceptibility and imperceptibility, of phenomena, these are inseparably bound together and exist in the same object.

The *Vajracchedikā* focuses our attention to the underlying true essence of mind which is an unchanging principle. The essence and phenomena of mind are inseparable. The perceptible and imperceptible phenomena are the manifestations of the mind in accordance with the number and nature of conditions. According to the teachings of the *Vajracchedikā*, it is a misconception to think or affirm that the Buddha comes into the world or goes because the blessed Buddha in his essential absolute nature is changeless and everlasting. This eternal conception of the Buddha is a salient feature of Mahāyāna, which is expounded by the *Vaipulya-sūtras* like the *Saddharma-Puṇḍarīka-Sūtra*. It is declared in the *Vajracchedikā*[40] that in the word "Buddha" every law is intelligently comprehended.

The *Dharma* and the *Saṅgha* are the two words which are of the great importance for a right apprehension of the teaching of the *Vajracchedikā*. In Buddhist terminology *dharma* means *saddharma*. All *dharmas* are subjective and differ from one another. That is why the *Vajracchedikā* teaches that all things are only "names" or "symbols" (*samjñās*)[41] and they are neither what they seem to be nor what they do not seem to be. For example "dust" is not dust because we cannot draw a line of demarcation between the smallest dust molecules and the smallest dust and the smallest gravel. Thus, they are nothing but names, which differentiate the individuality. Every name and every concept is merely a garb. This is what is meant by perfect wisdom in which nothing "not even the smallest thing is known or known to be known." One who realizes that he has attained the highest state does not believe either in an "idea" or a "name" or a "thing" or "an expression" or the "idea of no-thing." This metaphysical extreme skepticism is depicted throughout the *Vajracchedikā*.

Going ahead of Abhidhamma philosophy according to which, although there are no things but there are elements or *dharmas*, the Mahāyāna chiefly represented by the Prajñāpāramitā texts rejects all *dharmas*. According to Mahāyāna conception, there are neither *dharma* nor "non-

---

40. E. Conze (tr.), *The Diamond Sūtra*, p. 58.

41. F. Max Müller, *op. cit.*, Introduction, p. xv, fn. 1.

dharma." For example, according to the *Vajracchedikā*[42] to perceive "*dharma*" as "no-*dharma*" is the true perception. We come across incidental references about the doctrines of *karma* and the reincarnation in the *Vajracchedikā*. *Karma* is the law. Regarding the reincarnation the Buddha incidentally refers to his personal reminiscences one of which belongs to a distant period of five hundred incarnations when he was with Dīpaṅkara Buddha.

Both the idealistic as well as materialistic views are rejected in the *Vajracchedikā.* The *sūtra* contains the Buddha's denial of the reality of all predicable things such as ego, soul and all appearances, "merit" and even of "liberation" and "non-liberation." The *vajracchedikā* expounds the concept of a Bodhisattva who is seeker of enlightenment or an Enlightened Being. In order to become a Bodhisattva a spiritual aspirant should develop non-attachment to social ties and material possessions. He should treat all phenomenal existence as illusory.

One of the most paradoxical techniques of the *Vajracchedikā* is that it uses *dharma* as a kind of instrument, which should be left as a raft by a sailor after crossing the waters. Similar to a raft which is forsaken after it serves the purpose the vehicle or the doctrine is to be cast away when one reaches the other shore of enlightenment.[43] The rules of the doctrine are intended only for beginners and advanced people but they can be of no use to the enlightened except to serve him in his role of a teacher. For a person who has crossed the horizon beyond duality the whole scene of the two banks and the river between them is simply gone. According to the *Vajracchedikā*, there is

---

42. E. Conze (tr.), *The Diamond Sūtra*, pp. 34-36.

43. *Ibid.*

neither the stream nor the banks, nor the raft, nor an enlightened one etc. In other words there is neither *saṁsāra* nor *nirvāṇa*. The *saṁsāra* and *nirvāṇa* are considered as the ultimate pair of opposites. In truth they are unreal. That is why Christmas Humphreys asserts.[44] "We understand now why it is said that *nirvāṇa* is *saṁsāra*. . . on the relative side we see them as duality; on the higher plane we see the two as one." The transcendental wisdom of the Prajñāpāramitā is beyond the domain of opposites and dualities.

In fact truth is un-declarable and "emancipation of truth" is just the name given to it. Therefore, according to the *Vajracchedikā* all the designations such as the *arhant*, the Bodhisattva, or the Buddha are only names since there is no such condition as "attainment" or "perfect enlightenment." For example, it is stated in the *sūtra* that because no *dharma* is called "*arhant*" that is why he is called an "*arhant*."[45] Similarly "there are no beings to be liberated, because "in fact there are no beings at all."[46] There is no fundamental difference between one "who is and who is not a Buddha." A Buddha "knows" and the "non-Buddha" does not know that he is a Buddha." The absolute truth or the knowledge of absolute cannot be fully grasped because it is beyond conceptualisation and categorization.

Merit is a motive force, which propels us towards enlightenment and in order to strive fruitfully we are bound to wish to amass it. That's why the Buddha of *Vajracchedikā* expounds how merit should be derived from perfect wisdom. Gaining merit through perfect wisdom surpasses the merit

---

44. Christmas Humphreys, *The Buddhist Way of Life*, p. 153.
45. E. Conze (tr.), *The Diamond Sūtra*, p. 44.
46. *Ibid.*, pp. 25; 61-62.

one accumulates by all other pious acts. Therefore, it is said[47] that one accrues merit through learning, studying, reciting, copying, reading and writing of the Prajñāpāramitā texts. To hoard merit is better than to hoard money, titles, honour, etc. But from the standpoint of the doctrine of *śūnyatā* it is dangerous even to conceive spiritual gains by means of hoarding merit through perfect wisdom. The ultimate significance of all the above dialectical statements of the *Vajracchedikā* is to lead an aspirant to the goal of higher affirmation by contradicting simple direct statements. The essence of the dialectic is that what truth the Buddha had understood intuitively is known to none because truth is not language-bound and it can be known neither through sense-perception nor inference. The teaching of the Buddha is meant to use the same as an instrument or a means to grasp the wisdom beyond all conceptualisation.

The Mahāyāna is often called the Vehicle of *pāramitā*s, which a Bodhisattva should practise incessantly in order to become perfect for the sake of universal liberation. *Prajñā* is the mother of all *pāramitā*s or perfections. According to the *Vajracchedikā*,[48] none of the six perfections are to be regarded as perfections or *pāramitā*s and then only they are truly called the *pāramitā*s. Similarly the Buddha is not to be seen or understood by the possession of the marks of the superman, because in truth the Buddha is identified with *dharmakāyā*. That's why the *Vajracchedikā* states[49] that the "Tathāgatha is to be seen from no marks as marks." The reason of the above dialectic statement is that any statement contains the word "*I*" is ipso facto false because in the real world nothing corresponds to it.

---

47. *Ibid.*, p. 40.

48. *Ibid.*, pp. 26-28.

49. *Ibid.*, p. 28.

Ideal of Bodhisattva

The *Vajracchedikā* expounds the concept of bodhisattva. It provides us various salient features of a bodhisattva who differs from *arhant* ideal of Theravādins. The most essential feature of a bodhisattva is his great vow (*mahāpraṇidhāna*). Having aimed at Buddha ideal a bodhisattva undertakes *Bodhicittotpada*. Intellect and will are harmoniously integrated in the *Bodhicitta,* which consists of two stages in its development namely:

(i) *Bodhi Pranidhi Citta* (wherein a bodhisattva makes great resolve).

(ii) *Bodhi Prastāna Citta* (wherein he practises *pāramitā*s to attain perfection).

The sole aim of a bodhisattva is to help all sentient beings in reaching the other shore of Enlightenment. As Christmas Humphreys affirms[50]

> . . . the Bodhisattva is concerned in the first place with every deed of help which will bring salvation to all mankind.His Vow is paramount: Let others gain Enlightenment; I shall not enter *nirvāṇa* until the last blade of grass has entered Buddhahood.

Thus, a bodhisattva is he who benefits the world (*loka hita*), who keeps the world in happiness (*loka sukha*), who is compassionate for the world (*lokānukampa*). In order to become a bodhisattva a disciple on the path should cultivate non-attachment to social ties as well as material possessions. He should practise non-apprehension (*anupalabdhi*). He should treat all phenomenal existence as illusory. Such a one would not rest in any *dharma* including the Buddha-*dharma,* practised prior to one's reaching the goal of *nirvāṇa*. Thus a bodhisattva

50. Christmas Humphreys, *op. cit.*, p. 155.

should consider the *dharma* only as a raft to cross over the stream. As the Enlightened one says:

> My teaching of the Good Law is to be likened unto a raft. The Buddha teaching must be relinquished; how much more so mis-teaching.[51]

By the above saying it is clear that any kind of attachment to emptiness is a disease as much as attachment to existence. Further Śākyamuni teaches Subhūti that a bodhisattva should not entertain the idea of an ego-entity, a personality, a being or a separated individuality. In other words a bodhisattva is he who transcends all phenomenal distinctions. All the bodhisattvas should discipline their thoughts in the following manner. A Bodhisattva should not have a notion that he is going from *saṁsāra* to *nirvāṇa*. Besides he should not think that he is instrumental in taking other phenomenal beings to *nirvāṇa*. Thus, Śākyamuni Buddha taught it to Subhūti when he says:

> If a bodhisattva announces: I will liberate all living creatures, he is not rightly called a bodhisattva. Wherefore? Because, Subhūti, there is really no such condition as that called bodhisattvaship, because Buddha teaches that all things are devoid of selfhood, devoid of personality, devoid of entity and devoid of separate individuality.[52]

Secondly, a bodhisattva should be an *apradisti*. The doctrine of non-ego or no-soul which was the principal teaching of Buddha in early Buddhism was emphasised repeatedly in the *Vajracchedikā* for Buddha teaches to Subhūti:

---

51. A.F. Price: *The Diamond Sūtra*, trd. from Chinese, p. 31; E. Conze (tr.), *The Diamond Sūtra*, p. 34.

52. A.F. Price, *Diamond Sūtra*, Eng. tr. p. 53; E. Conze (tr.), *The Diamond Sūtra*, p. 25.

> I must liberate all living beings yet when all have been liberated, verily not any one is liberated.[53]

Another virtue to be cultivated by a bodhisattva is that he should not cherish the concepts of name and form identity. As the Buddha states to his disciple Subhūti:

> When the Rājah of Kaliṅga, mutilated my body, I was at that time free from the ideas of an ego-entity, a personality, a being and a separated individuality. Wherefore? Because then when my limbs were cut away piece by piece, had I been bound by the distinctions aforesaid, feelings of anger and hatred would have been aroused within me.[54]

The Buddha of *Vajracchedikā* declares that the six perfections such as *dāna, śīla, vīrya*, etc. are merely names but not distinctive ideas. For instance the bodhisattva without being conscious of giving something to others should perform charity (*dāna*). In other words, guided by perfect wisdom a bodhisattva should have "no perception of others, no perception of a gift." Thus Śākyamuni Buddha repeats the teaching of Lord Kṛṣṇa in the *Bhagavad-Gītā*.

> (But) work alone is your proper business, never the fruits (it may produce): let not your motive be the fruit of works nor your attachment to (mere) worklessness.[55]
>
> *karmaṇy ev 'ādhikāras te mā phaleṣu kadācana, mā karma-phala-hetur bhūr mā te saṅgo 'stvakarmaṇi*

Similar to the above teaching Śākyamuni instructs Subhūti:

---

53. *Ibid.*, p. 52, E. Conze (tr.), *The Diamond Sūtra*, p. 57.
54. *Ibid.*, p. 44, E. Conze (tr.), *The Diamond Sūtra*, p. 54.
55. See. *Bhagavad-Gītā*, Chap. II. St. 47; R.C. Zaehner (tr.), *The Bhagavad-Gītā*, p. 145.

> Subhūti, bodhisattvas who achieve merit should not be fettered with desire for rewards. Thus it is said that the rewards of merit are not received.[56]

Thus, all virtues including six perfections will no more be felt as such and will transform into a natural attitude of spiritual freedom in the acts of a bodhisattva. Contrary to other orthodox systems of the ancient Indian thought such as *nyāya* and *sāṁkhya* who maintain an unifying link "self" or *ātman* *Vajracchedikā* advocates the doctrine of non-self, by denying the self, being, soul or person as permanent entities in conformity with the original doctrine of Śākyamuni. Rightly observing the above fact Bhikṣu Saṅgharakśita asserts:

> Whereas, the original teaching starts from the "self" the Mahāyāna starts from the "non-self" . . . the purpose of both teachings is to make sure that the practice of the *dharma* functions not as a hindrance but as a help to the attainment of the transcendental path." Both, therefore, insist upon a simultaneous observance of the absolute Truth and the relative Truth.[57]

Thus, the Enlightened Śākyamuni in the *Vajracchedikā* instructs Subhūti that bodhisattvas should leave all phenomenal distinctions and awaken the thought of the consummation of incomparable enlightenment by not allowing their minds to depend upon notions evoked by the different sensory qualities. Hence a bodhisattva should not regard the appearances of things as a basis of exercising his *Pāramitājñāna*. He should grasp the essential idea that elements of *saṁsāra* are illusory and transient like a morning star, a water-bubble, a lightning-flash, a flickering lamp and a dream.

---

56. A.F. Price, (tr.) *The Diamond Sūtra*, p. 69; E. Conze (tr.), *The Diamond Sūtra*, pp. 55-57.

57. Bhikṣu Saṅgharakshita: *A Survey of Buddhism*, pp. 442-43.

The Truth of perfection of Transcendental Wisdom taught by the Buddha in the *Vajracchedikā* is ungraspable (*agrāhya*). It is free from all dualism, beyond all conceptualization and categorization. It is incommunicable through language. Hence W.Y. Evans Wentz rightly asserts[58]

> In the "Full" awakening from the Dream of Existence, upon the attaining of Buddhahood, nothing is either lost or gained, there is only the realization of what has ever been beyond the grasp of mortal mind.

One of the most important teachings of the *Vajracchedikā* is that Truth is incomplete and relative at pragmatic level, while the Perfection of Transcendental Wisdom is absolutistic in character. Paradoxically, the Buddha of *Vajracchedikā* concludes that there is neither the attainer of transcendental wisdom, nor the attained; *prajñā* is beyond the *dharma* and non-*dharma*, subject and the object. All names and concepts are mere garbs by which the Reality is shrouded. Illumination means to understand that the gulf between *saṁsāra* and *nirvāṇa* is delusion. Therefore, to an awakened one who becomes one with the Tathāgata, there is neither the notion of the saviour nor saved, neither the preacher (Buddha) nor the doctrine (*dharma*) nor the practitioner (*saṅgha*), neither the world (*saṁsāra*) nor illusion (ignorance) nor *nirvāṇa* (labelled reality). That is the reason why the Enlightened one teaches Subhūti that just as the states of *srotāpanna* (stream-entrant) *sakridagāmin* (once-to-be-reborn), *anāgāmin* (non-returner), *arhant* (perfectly enlightened) are mere designations and these winners have no notion of their attainments. A bodhisattva would not feel that he is an "Attainer of Bodhisattva-hood." Hence addressing ven. Subhūti the Lord says:[59]

---

58. A.F. Price, (tr.), *Diamond Sūtra*, See W.Y. Evans-Wentz's Foreword, pp. 16-17.
59. E. Conze, (tr.), *The Diamond Sūtra*, pp. 25, 38, 43.

> If in a bodhisattva the notion of a "being" should take place, he could not be called a Bodhi-being, in whom the notion of a self or of a being should take place, or the notion of a living soul or of a person.

As in all Mahāyāna sūtras, the bodhisattva of *Vajracchedikā* too is a virtual Buddha who fully comprehends the nirvānic essence of *saṁsāra*. He is the perfect being who establishes the connection with phenomena (*saṁsāra*) by the element of "*mahākaruṇā*," which is an ontological link between pain and felicity. The ideal of bodhisattva in *Vajracchedikā* is a principle "*nirvāṇa* present in *saṁsāra*" who aims at "cosmic perfection." Thus, it can be said that a bodhisattva depicted in *Vajracchedikā* is an embodiment of *prajñā* and *karuṇā* who remains as the principle of mediation between the absolute (*śūnya*) and the phenomena (*saṁsāra*) whose one look dwells in the Absolute (*taṭhatā*) and the other rests in the Phenomena (*saṁsāra*) of sentient beings. As T.R.V. Murti rightly puts it:

> Buddha and bodhisattva, who models himself on him are thus amphibious beings with one foot in the absolute and the other in phenomena.[60]

Characteristics of the Conditioned Phenomena

The *Vajracchedikā* enunciates the unreality of all phenomena. According to this *sūtra*, *nirvāṇa* and *saṁsāra*, although appear as the ultimate pair of opposites, their distinction is unreal. Truth can be realised only in the transcendental states beyond the domains of opposites. Truth is "undeclarable" and an "emancipation of truth" is the mere name given to it. The key to the supreme knowledge is given in this treatise. Whoever takes four lines from a discourse of this *sūtra* either by reciting or by writing or by retaining or by practising for the benefit

---

60. T.P.V. Murti, *The Central Philosophy of Buddhism*, p. 264.

of others will acquire greater merit than one who fills up the countless worlds with the seven treasures and gives all of them in charity.[61] As the teaching expounded in this *sūtra* cannot be directly explained, by means of the following verse the conditioned nature of all phenomena is taught.

> as stars, a fault of vision, as a lamp,
> a mock-show, dewdrops, or a bubble,
> a dream, a lightning flash, or cloud,
> so should one view what is conditioned[62]

All the above similies mentioned in the above verse suggest in a metaphysical way that all elements of *saṁsāra* should be viewed as transient and illusory. The meaning of all these similes is elaborately explained as follows:

(1) ***Stars***: Stars are unattainable as they are distant and unreachable. Similarly all *dharma*s are un-possessed. The metaphor of stars can be further interpreted as follows: when compared to the infinity of space, stars are very insignificant. The things of the world are seen only when the darkness is dispelled, just as stars are seen only in the absence of sun.[63] The word "star" is also explained as "meteor" which has only a short life.

(2) ***Fault of vision***: Ignorance is compared to a fault of vision which may also mean darkness, blindness resulted from cataract. Just as a cataract overpowers the eyes, so too ignorance overpowers beings. Ignorance has a triple dimension[64] namely intellectual, emotional and volitional. An ignorant man sees the

61. E. Conze, (tr.), *The Diamond Sūtra,* p. 50.

62. *Ibid.*, p. 68.

63. *Ibid.*

64. *Ibid.*, pp. 68-69.

world which is a hallucination, just as a jaundiced eye sees the phenomena as yellowish. For instance a person afflicted with "timira" a disease sees hairs in his alms-bowl.

(3) ***Lamp***: The simile of the lamp illustrates "two aspects" of the world (i) just as a lamp burns as long as its fuel lasts, the world continues to exist so long as we have craving (ii) just as lamps are liable to be blown out easily by the wind, so too all conditioned things are very easily disturbed by others. This reveals the fact that all conditioned *dharma*s are precarious.[65]

(4) ***Mock-show***: The phenomenal world is compared to a mock-show or a magical illusion. In contrast to the absolute reality a magical show deceives and deludes the ignorant beings.[66] Great philosophers like Nāgārjuna and Vasubandhu respectively emphasized the point that all conditioned things are produced by ignorance. Although ignorance is unreal it is the condition for all kinds of activity. For example musical instruments conjured up by magic are empty and deceptive and have no objective basis.

(5) ***Dewdrops***: Just as the dewdrops which depend on climate, have only momentary existence and are quickly evaporated under the rays of the sun, so also the phenomenal things are evanescent.[67]

(6) ***Bubble***: According to the Buddhist tradition, just as the bubble which is only an unsubstantial entity and bursts off quickly, so too, all experience is momentary[68]

---

65. p. 69.
66. *Ibid.*
67. *Ibid.*
68. *Ibid.*, p. 70.

(as the bubble). Further pleasure and pain are quickly liable to disappear (similar to the bubble) depending upon three factors namely enjoyer, the enjoyable thing and enjoyment.

(7) ***Dream***: When compared to the awakening of the enlightened being, the normal human experience of a human being is as unreal as a dream. According to Nāgārjuna, a Mādhyamika philosopher, even though a dream is unreal, yet for the dreamer the experience of the dream is real. The dreamer after he wakes up recognises his foolishness for he believed the unreal as real. Similarly when a person comes out from the dreaming state of fettered existence, he understands the unreality of the "conditioned phenomena." Further just as a dreamer sees an object where there is actually nothing, so also an ignorant man who dwells in the world of objects believes its objects and makes distinctions such as "I" and "mine."[69]

(8) ***Lightning flash***: The simile of the lightning flash indicates that like the lightning flash in the cloudy sky, which is quite "momentary" and transcient, so also each event or occurrence in the phenomenal world is very brief and short lived.[70]

(9) ***Cloud***: The *Vajracchedikā* expounds the Buddha's teaching which advises a wise man to look at the worldly phenomena in the same spirit as one watches the summer clouds which continuously change their shapes. Similarly the transformations of the worldly objects are transcient and unreal[71] both from the subjective as well as the objective view-points.

---

69. *Ibid.*

70. *Ibid.*

71. *Ibid.*

SADDHARMA PUṆḌARĪKA SŪTRA

Introduction

The *Saddharma Puṇḍarīka* or the *Lotus of true Law* is a book of Indian origin and high imagination. It belongs to the group of apocalyptic literature. It is one of the *Nava Dharma*s or nine famous sacred texts of Nepal[72] that belong to the *Mahāvaipulya Sūtra* literature of Mahāyāna that survive today, the others being the *Aṣṭasāharikā Prajñāpāramitā*, the *Daśabhūmika*, the *Samādhirāja*, the *Laṅkāvatāra*, the *Gaṇḍavyūha*, the *Suvarṇaprabhāsa*, the *Lalitavistara*, and the *Tathāgataguhyaka* or the *Guhyasamāja*. The *Saddharma Puṇḍarīka* is called as *Mahāvaipulya Sūtra* by its internal textual evidence.[73] It is one among the 97 Sanskrit texts quoted by Śāntideva in his *Śikṣāsamuccaya*. It is the most universally authoritative and favourite treatise of the Buddhists in Far-East. It is the most popular Buddhist religious scripture whose manuscripts are available not only in India but also in Tibet, Nepal and Central Asia. Manuscripts of the *Sūtra* are mainly classified into 3 groups, viz. (i) Nepalese version, (ii) Gilgit or Kashmir version, (iii) Central Asian version.

The Sanskrit originals of *Saddharma Puṇḍarīka* are acquired from Nepal, Tibet, Kashmir and Central Asia. The following are the Sanskrit editions[74] of the *Saddharma Puṇḍarīka*:

(1) Devanāgarī edition by H. Kern and Bunyu Nanjio, published in Bibliotheca Buddhica, St. Petersburg (1908-12).

---

72. H. Kern (tr.), *The Saddharma Puṇḍarīka Sūtra or The Lotus of the True Law*, see Introduction, p. ix.

73. *Ibid.*, p. x.

74. H. Nakamura, Indian Buddhism, p. 183, fn. 4; R.P. Dvivedi, *Bauddha Sanskṛta Kāvya Sameekṣa*, p. 343.

(2) Romanized and revised text of the above ed. by U. Wogihara and C. Tsuchida, published from Tokyo (1934-35).

(3) Devanāgarī edition revised by Nalinaksha Dutt, pub. from Asiatic Society, Calcutta (1953).

(4) Devanāgarī edition ed. by P.L. Vaidya, pub. from Darbhanga (1960).

(5) Devanāgarī edition edited by Ram Mohan Das, Bihar Rastra Bhasa Parishad, Bihar (1966).

There are as many as 17 complete and partial Chinese translations[75] of the *Saddharma-Puṇḍarīka-Sūtra*. Of the above there are three extant complete Chinese translations the oldest of which is ascribed to *Dharmārakṣa* of the Western Tsin dynasty (265-316 CE). It is followed by Kumārajīva's translation of later Tshin dynasty (384-417 CE) which corresponds to its Tibetan, and the third translation was done by Gnanagupta and Dharmagupta of Sui dynasty (601 CE). Of the above, whereas the first two translations consist of twenty-eight chapters each, the last bears twenty-seven chapters and there is varied opinion regarding their dates of composition.[76] In L. Hurvitz's opinion, of the above Kumārajīva's Sanskrit version is considered as the best. It is translated into Japanese[77] by Sotoku Taishi (615 CE),[78] B. Nanjio and Hokei Idzumi (Hokekyo, 1913), into modern Japanese by Y. Iwamoto and Yukio Sakamoto (1962, 1964) and Mitsuyoshi Saigusa (in 3 vols., Tokyo, 1974) besides an incomplete Japanese translation by Seiren Matsunami and

---

75. H. Nakamura, *Indian Buddhism*, p. 185.

76. But according to K.H. Potter Dharmarakṣa and Kumārajīva's translations are respectively dated as 286 CE and 405-46 CE, See K.H. Potter, *Encyclopaedia of Indian Philosophies*, vol. VIII, p. 739.

77. H. Nakamura, *op. cit.*, p. 183, fn.4.

78. R.P. Dvivedi, *op. cit.*, p. 344.

others (1975). It is translated into Tibetan by Surendrabodhi and Sna-nam-ye-ses-sole.

The Sanskrit text of the *Saddharma Puṇḍarīka* has been translated into French by M.E. Burnouf (1852) and into German by F.W.K. Müller and W. Radoff. It is translated into English by W.E. Soothill (Oxford, 1930), H. Kern (SBE. vol. xxi, 1884), Senchu Murano (Japan, 1964), Buno Kato, Yoshiro Tamura and Kojiro Miyasaka (Tokyo, 1971, 1975), Leon Hurvitz (New York, 1976). It is translated into Hindi by Ram Mohan Das (Bihar, 1966). There are two commentaries on this *sūtra* composed by Vasubandhu (550-600 CE) and Shotoku Taishi. Vasubandhu's Sanskrit commentary of this *sūtra* was translated into Chinese by Ratnamani and Bodhiruchi. According to Paramardha, more than 50 Indian scholars had either commented upon or elucidated the *Lotus Sūtra*, but only Vasubandhu's commentary was translated into Chinese.

Theodore De Bary asserts that in the whole Buddhist canonical literature the *Lotus Sūtra* is "a major religious scripture of enduring importance . . . a comprehensive and effective statement of the teachings of Mahāyāna Buddhism, most inspiring for its religious imagery and for its dramatic presentation of those teachings in a form readily appreciated by millions of Buddhists in China, Japan and Korea."[79] The *Lotus Sūtra* is one of the most influential of Mahāyāna scriptures which occupies a very important place in Buddhist *saṅgha* throughout Far East. While pointing out its importance Daisaku Ikeda holds

> the fact that in India, China and Japan there are more commentaries on this text than on any other in the canon offers further proof of its enormous importance.[80]

---

79. see W.M. Theodore De Bary's Foreword in Leon Hurvitz, *Scripture of the Lotus Blossom of the Fine Dharma*, p. vii.

80. Daisaku Ikeda, *Buddhism the First Millennium*, p. 112.

In Far Eastern countries, the *Lotus Sūtra* has become an object of reverence because it is considered to be consisting of the final doctrine and supreme teaching of the Buddha. The Tendai and Nichiren Buddhist sects depend entirely on this *sūtra*. The *Lotus Sūtra* has influenced Japanese Buddhist teaching in other Buddhist sects as well.

As regards the probable date of the composition of the *Saddharma Puṇḍarīka* a large number of thinkers of both east and west such as P.L. Vaidya, Baladev Upadhyay, Nalinaksha Dutt, G.C. Pandey, Acharya Narendra Dev, Suryakantha Sastry, Sukumari Bhattacharji, A.B. Keith, M. Winternitz unanimously contend[81] that it is composed sometime around 1. *c.* CE. This *sūtra* seems to belong to late first century CE. as its first Chinese translation appeared in the 2. *c.* CE. According to H. Nakamura,[82] prototype of this *sūtra* currently available to us was produced in 1. *c.* CE. K. Fuse holds[83] that the Sanskrit original which consists of 27 chapters was in existence during 150 CE. H. Ui asserts[84] that the first 22 chapters of the *Saddharma Puṇḍarīka* was in existence before 100 CE. Winternitz[85] presumes that based on Nāgārjuna's duration of life, we may infer that the *sūtra* was in existence by the end of 1. *c.* CE. According to scholars[86] like G. Ono, L. Poussin and Ch. Humphreys this *sūtra* was completed about the end of the 2. *c.* CE. F. Edgerton opines[87] that from the literary point of view the *Lotus Sūtra* is

81. R.C. Dvivedi, *op. cit.*, p. 344; S. Bhattacharji, *op. cit.*, p. 150.
82. H. Nakamura, *op. cit.*, p. 186.
83. *Ibid.*, p. 186, fn. 17.
84. *Ibid.*, p. 186, fn. 18.
85. M. Winternitz, *History of Indian Literature*, vol. II, p. 304.
86. H. Nakamura, *op. cit.*, p. 186, fn. 20; Christmas Humphreys, *A Popular Dictionary of Buddhism*, p. 161.
87. F. Edgerton, *Buddhist Hybrid Sanskrit Language and literature*, p. 36.

one of the best in the entire Buddhist hybrid Sanskrit literature and the last seven among its 27 chapters appear to be the later editions. According to H. Kern,[88] also the chapters xxi-xxvi of the *Lotus Sūtra* are of later growth. S. Bhattacharya[89] thinks that the text of the *Lotus Sūtra* has two recensions of which the older recension consist of chaps i-xx and xxvii and the later recension consists of chaps. xxii-xxv.

Central Teachings

Scholars like Leon Hurvitz opine[90] that the lotus of the *Fine Law* represents a Buddhist tendency that calls itself Mahāyāna, apparently signifying the "great course." The *Saddharma Puṇḍarīka* is a major *Mahāyāna Sūtra* which is glorified as the supreme, the most sublime of the *sūtra*s delivered by the lord and is celebrated as the crown jewel (*siromaṇi*) and the most eminent of all *sūtras*.[91] The essential doctrines of the *Lotus Sūtra* are as below:

(i) The Buddha is not to be delineated in time and space. It establishes the *dharmakāya* conception of the Buddha in contrast to the early Buddhist conception of the series of Buddhas who will be similar in their career, preach the same *dharma* and become extinct after some time.

(ii) The *Lotus Sūtra* preaches universal salvation as against self-salvation by acknowledging potential Buddhahood in all sentient beings.

---

88. H Kern, *op. cit.*, Introduction, p. xxi.

89. Sukumari Bhattacharji, *Buddhist Hybrid Sanskrit Literature*, p. 43.

90. Leon Hurvitz (tr.), *Scripture of the Lotus Blossom of the Fine Dharma*, Preface. p. xvi.

91. H. Kern, *op. cit.*, Introduction. p. xxix, fn. 1; chap. XIII, St. 53-54; chap. XXII, pp. 386-88.

(iii) The attainment of Buddhahood is the highest and only form of salvation, which is known as the "*sarvajñatā jñāna*" or real *nirvāṇa*.

(iv) The *Lotus Sūtra* hinges on the point of salvation by one vehicle (*ekayāna*), which is Buddhayāna or Bodhisattvayāna.

(v) The Lotus depicts bodhisattvas as enlighteners and compassionate saviours of mankind who by their great vow postpone their enlightenment till all sentient beings attain final *nirvāṇa*.

(vi) The highest salvation or Buddhahood can be attained by means of faith and devotion.

Ideal of the Tathāgata

According to the *Lotus Sūtra,* in fact the Buddha is transcendent, immanent and eternal *dharmakāya* who resembles the God of theistic religions. Śākyamuni Gautama is one of his expressions in one of the infinite worlds. In the *Lotus Sūtra* as well as in Pāli literature the Buddha is referred as "Devāti Deva"[92] (the paramount god of gods). In the *Lotus Sūtra* Gautama Buddha is identified with the one who was roused to maturity from the eternity. The fact that the Buddha had obtained *bodhi* from eternity is indicated by His words in the *sūtra time immemorial and the very beginning,* etc. Not only has he lived an infinite number of aeons in the past but also he is to live forever. He never enters *nirvāṇa*. In the *Lotus Sūtra* the Buddha most solemnly declares that he had reached *bodhi* an immense time ago not as people fancy at Gayā. Common people fancy that Buddha enters *nirvāṇa,* but in reality he only makes a show of it. In other words, the Buddha is the self-

---

92. *Ibid.,* pp. xxvi-xxvii.

born (*svayambhu*), the chief saviour of all, who only appears to be born in the world, strives for *nirvāṇa* and entered into it. In reality the Eternal Buddha always dwells on Mount Vulture peak (Gridhrakūṭa) speaks from eternity, to eternity repeatedly appears in the world guaranteeing Buddhahood to all beings through his immensely potent skill-in-means (*upāya kauśalya*). Thus according to the *Lotus Sūtra*, paradoxically no Buddha has ever come into existence to enlighten the world with Buddhist teachings. Thus, the *Lotus Sūtra* throughout the text represents the Buddha as "superhuman."

In this *Sūtra*, Buddha is depicted as the "*Supreme-Being, Almighty all-wise.*" Philosophically speaking, similar to Lord Kṛṣṇa of the *Bhagavad-Gītā*, the Buddha of the *Saddharma Puṇḍarīka* is *Puruṣothama Paramātman*, the highest *Brahman* and also the *Supreme Mind*. He was responsible for the spiritual progress of all the bodhisattvas. Thus he made identical with the Ādi Buddha.

Distinguishing Lord Kṛṣṇa from the Buddha, Kern opines that unlike the former who is an incarnated person, the latter is only "an ideal and a *personification* and not a person." Kern[93] compares Śākyamuni with the *Punyāpekṣita muni* spoken in *Manu* (viii. 91) who is the beholder of good and evil and also with the *Eternal Kūtaṣṭha* (immutable reality) of Vedānta. According to the interpretations of Soothill, a celebrated scholar, the lotus is the metaphor for the universe as well as the *nidus* of the soul since from the spiritual lotus-flower springs a *soul* or *life*. The eternal Buddha is the mind behind the lotus. The eternal Buddha conception of the *Lotus Sūtra* resembles the eternal son-ship of Christianity and similar assertion of Lord Kṛṣṇa in the *Gītā* who proclaims to have taught *yoga* to the Sun god. W.E. Soothill infers that the Buddha is omnipotent

93. *Ibid.*, p. xxviii.

on the basis of the latter's supreme power to summon all beings to the assembly and shake all creation at his will. Similarly the omnipresence of the Buddha is evident from his supreme power to penetrate into all worlds and since he can appear anywhere at his will. We come across a number of parables of the *Lotus Sūtra* wherein we find that the Buddha is ready to guide and awaken them from their dogmatic slumber of ignorance through his teaching of "*Saddharma*." He persuades all sentient beings similar to a good compassionate father (in the Parable of Burning House who rescues his children) and similar to a highly learned expert physician (in the parable of blind man and the physician). The Tathāgata's message is meant for all similar to the rays of the Sun and the Moon in the sky and the "Great cloud" which pours down the life giving rain on all kinds of plants and trees without any discrimination.

Doctrine of Universal Salvation

The *Lotus Sūtra* enunciates that all beings are capable of realising the state of Buddha-hood attained by Gautama or Śākyamuni for the first time. In contrast to the early Buddhist goals of *śrāvaka* and the pratyeka Buddha who aim only at self-salvation the Buddha of the *Lotus Sūtra* preaches universal salvation. He then proceeds to narrate parables and analogies to illustrate how among the three vehicles of the *śrāvaka*s, and the pratyeka Buddhas, the vehicle of bodhisattvas or Buddhas of Mahāyāna the last one are far superior and the best. The Buddha of the *Lotus Sūtra* has proclaimed the ultimate salvation of Buddha-hood for all sentient beings by assuring the final enlightenment even to the demons and the inhabitants of the hells. Because every sentient being is a potential Buddha, all sentient beings are guaranteed Buddha-hood.

Buddha-hood as the highest goal of Perfection

The *Lotus Sūtra* appears to be the eternal gospel and final revelation given by the Buddha. It is considered as the highest among all expositions of the *dharma* of Śākyamuni Buddha. The *Lotus of the True Law* is variously described as:[94]

> "the king of all *sūtras*;" it is like the Sumeru among the elevations at the cardinal points; like the moon among the luminaries; the Sun who dispels all darkness, like Indra of the gods it is chief of the *sūtras*, like the Brahma the king of gods, it plays a father's role of all beings; like a Bodhisattva who is superior to *śrāvakas* and pratyeka Buddhas, it is superior to all *sūtras*; moreover it saves all beings from fear and all suffering; it serves like a tank for the thirsty; like a fire for the sufferers from cold; like a clothing for the naked; like a caravan leader for the merchants; like a mother for her children; like a boat for those who cross the waters; like a lamp in the darkness; like a jewel for the seekers of wealth and like an ocean for the rivers.

The teachings of the Buddha in the *Lotus Sūtra* were preached during the second turn of the Wheel of the *dharma* (*dvitīya dharma chakra pravartana*). The Buddha of the *Lotus Sūtra* is the universal father of all worlds who always endeavours to put an end to all fear, despondency, distress, ignorance and gloom of all sentient beings and makes an effort of leading them to the goal of perfection. The Buddha of the *Lotus Sūtra* explains why he is making the greater revelation of *dharma* than before. He employs a tactical method of expedience which gradually prepares the disciples of lower grades such as arhats and pratyeka Buddhas for receiving the higher wisdom of "Tathāgata-knowledge" (*Tathāgata-jñāna*). The Buddha-vehicle, which is the supreme of all the three vehicles, is open to all.

---

94. *Ibid.*, chap. XXII, pp. 386-88.

Doctrine of One Vehicle (Ekayāna)

This is one of the important concepts of Mahāyāna Buddhist philosophy. *Ekayāna* is one of the significant doctrines propounded by the Buddha, as expounded by him in the *Saddharma-Puṇḍarīka-Sūtra* for the first time. According to *The Lotus Sūtra,* the Buddha's mission in this world is to establish that there is only one vehicle.[95] According to B. Shio,[96] the origin of the doctrine of the single vehicle can be found in early Buddhist scriptures.The *Lotus Sūtra*'s emphasis on the uniqueness of the single vehicle reminds us of the "one truth"[97] preached by the Buddha in the *Sutta-Nipāta*:

> For Truth is one, and there is no second, concerning which one being might quarrel with others. They themselves, moreover, groan out a variety of truths and for this reason the ascetic monks do not speak of one alone.[98]

According to this *sūtra,* there are not many paths to attain the ultimate state of enlightenment known as the knowledge of "Tathāgatha" (Tathāgatha-*jñāna*). It is further said that the three paths, viz. the path of the *śrāvaka*s, the path of the pratyeka Buddhas and the path of bodhisattvas, preached by the Buddha should not be mistaken as diverse ways. The Buddha preaches them to the people of diverse dispositions

---

95. (i) *ekamaevāham sāriputra yānamārabhya sattavānām dharmam desayāmi yadidam buddhayānam* ।
na kinci sāriputra dvitīyam va trutīyam vā yānam samvidyate ॥

ii) *ekam idam yāna dvitīya nāsti;*

iii) . . . *nāsti yānatrayam kincid ekayānamihāstitu* — Prof. H. Kern and Prof. B. Nanjio (ed.), *Saddharma Puṇḍarīka,* pp. 40, 49, 143.

96. H. Nakamura, *op. cit.*, p. 189.

97. Fuzita Kotatsu, "One Vehicle or Three?" *Journal of Indian Philosophy,* 3, pp. 82.

98. *Ibid.*, p. 117.

of countless beings who are caught in the cycle of transmigration. The *Lotus Sūtra* illustrates the doctrine of one vehicle (*ekayāna*) of salvation in which the Buddha abides and with which he saves all sentient beings. The Buddha does not teach three vehicles, viz. The Vehicles of Śrāvakas, Pratyeka Buddhas and the Bodhisattvas although these are some of the many forms of exposition designed by his expediency to train the beings who have diverse mental inclinations. Buddhas of all spheres of the past, present and future uniformly teach a single vehicle on account of the diversity of tastes and mental calibres of beings.[99] They mention three vehicles, in spite of the fact that there is only one vehicle. According to Shinjo Suguro,[100] in the *Lotus Sūtra ekayāna* refers to the Buddha vehicle (Buddhayāna) and the bodhisattvayāna means one of the three vehicles. As a corollary to the doctrine of one vehicle, it is stated that just like one vehicle, there is only one True- *nirvāṇa* (not two or three), which is defined as the realisation or understanding of the "sameness" of all laws (*tathatā*). The summum bonum of all beings is not *nirvāṇa* realised by Arahants, Pratyeka Buddhas and bodhisattvas (as described in the early Buddhist teachings) who only destroy their mental and physical impurities (*kleśabandha vinirmuktaḥ*), the irreversible bodhisattvas (*avaivarttikā*s), who have realised only non-existence of individuality (*pudgala-śūnyatā*). The above-mentioned are those who have only accomplished the limited vision of truth like the "blind man" (in the parable of blind man and the physician) whose sight is restored by the great physician (i.e., Tathāgata). The Nirvānic attainments of Śrāvakayāna followers, viz. the *Arhant*s and Pratyeka Buddhas

---

99. *na sānti kaśyapa trīṇi yānāni kevaḷamanyonyacharitāḥ sattvaḥ* ।
tena trīṇi yānaṁ Prajñāpyatyute — Kern and Nanjio, *op. cit.*, p. 132.

100. See H. Nakamura, *op. cit.*, p. 189, fn. 5.

are only a temporary repose and not a final rest. Just as the clay of the different pots containing milk, curd, *ghee*, etc. is identical, so also, there is only "one *nirvāṇa*" but not two or three as it is often supposed is the teaching imparted by the Buddha to venerable Kasyapa. Moreover, the diverse means indicate the skill-in-means of the Buddha who out of great compassion imparts the same teaching to all beings by helping them in understanding the supreme teaching of the Buddha's doctrine of *ekayāna* is illustrated by a number of parables[101] such as the "parable of burning house," the "parable of blind man and the physician" "the parable of physician and sons" the "parable of the great cloud," etc.

Role of Bodhisattvas as Enlighteners and Saviours

This *sūtra* depicts the Bodhisattva as the spiritual son of the Buddha. There are several bodhisattvas such as Mañjuśrī, Avalokiteśvara, Samantabhadra, who are endowed with wisdom and compassion. They actively participate in assisting the Buddha and protecting the faithful. They act as supporters, protectors, reciters, preachers, promulgators of the *Lotus Sūtra*. They also play the role of redeemers, enlighteners and saviours of suffering humanity and as the compassionate fellowman. They are found as the objects of contemplation and devotion.[102] Although they are fit for the Buddha-hood, they withdraw from liberation; they will not enter into the final *nirvāṇa*. The *Lotus Sūtra* refers to the great and ordinary bodhisattvas in this and other similar worlds. This *sūtra* also mentions about the future Buddha known as Maitreya the Messiah who is going to restore the *dharma*.

---

101. H. Kern (tr.), *op. cit.*, pp. 119-121, 123.

102. *Ibid.*, p. 416, sts. 25-26.

Doctrine of Salvation by Faith and Devotion

The *dharmakāyā* conception of the Buddha which implies an ever enduring personality, the Ādi-Buddha as primordial reality, the *nirvāṇa* and sambhogakāya Buddhas who are endowed with infinite wisdom (*prajñāpāramitā*) and great compassion (*mahākaruṇā*) led to the conception of the Buddha of the *Saddharma Puṇḍarīka* as the highest object of reverence and worship. In contrast to early Buddhist teachings which are only the interim doctrines meant for *śrāvaka*s and pratyeka Buddhas who are not ready to receive the complete truth, the Buddha of the *Lotus Sūtra* reveals the final truth, viz. that the final *nirvāṇa*/liberation cannot be obtained by self-discipline and holy works but only by faith and invocation. This has remarkable resemblance to the Christian doctrine of Fatherhood of God and salvation by faith. It is based on the philosophical presupposition that one's irreversible faith in the Buddhas and bodhisattvas' saving power will transform the force of *karma* exercised through their transfer of merit. Those who receive the gospel of the *Lotus Sūtra* wherever they may be, even in the hells shall escape and obtain the glorious Buddha-realms which are infinite in variety, number and splendour. Even though ultimately every one is guaranteed the perfect enlightenment, meanwhile, whoever is endowed with faith and devotion attains the appropriate Buddha-realm in accordance with one's merit. Thus, the doctrine of salvation by faith and devotion[103] to the Buddhas and bodhisattvas as the essential and only means to attain Buddha-hood is advocated in the *Lotus Sūtra*. Some scholars like A.K. Warder, E.J. Thomas and Kenneth K.S. Ch'en hold that this *sūtra* is mainly devotional and avoids philosophical

103. V.V.S. Saibaba, *Saddharma Puṇḍarīka Sūtra — A Devotional Buddhist treatise*, Young East, vol. 1, no. 4, pp. 27-33.

aspects by taking for granted all the Mahāyāna Buddhist philosophical truths.

Philosophical Significance of the Parables

According to scholars like D.T. Suzuki, *upāya* means "expedient" or "stratagem" or "device" or "craft," which has a technical sense in Buddhist thought. *Upāya* is used in contrast to *prajñā* or intelligence and it is synonymous with *karuṇā* (love) towards all beings. In Mahāyāna Buddhist philosophy "*prajñā*" is understood as the one universal, which represents the principle of sameness. *Upāya* is understood as the many being the principle of manifoldness (*nānātva*). Although there is one religion namely religion of truth, there are many ways or devices all issuing from the *dharmakāyā* and are equally efficient to lead all sentient beings towards the goal of supreme enlightenment.

The concept of *upāya* is rendered as "skilful means" or "skill-in-means." It springs from a clear perception of a truth of *śūnyatā*. The "skill-in-means" cohabits with the intuition or *prajñā* in the mind of a bodhisattva. One of the chief characteristics of Mahāyāna is that *prajñā*, *upāya* and *karuṇā* are linked together.

According to the philosophy of Prajñāpāramitā, when the mind of the bodhisattva abides with perfect conformity with *pāramitā*s or perfections, he becomes benevolent towards all sentient beings out of great compassion. Being endowed with a spiritual insight a bodhisattva perceives suffering in the whole universe. He is intensely interested in the upliftment and progress of all the sentient beings towards perfection and the goal of the knowledge of Tathāgatha. Thus there is an intrinsic relationship between the all-knowledge or omniscience of Tathāgatha, *prajñā* or intuition or insight into the true nature of things, great compassion or *karuṇā*, which springs from the former and *upāya* or the skilful means by which a Bodhisattva helps for the salvation of all sentient beings.

The Buddha of the *Lotus Sūtra* elucidates to venerable Sāriputra that all his teachings of the Law have no other purpose or goal except the attainment of supreme enlightenment. All the Buddha's teachings are meant to rouse beings to the Bodhisattva's conduct. The Buddha resorts to several teachings, ideas, directions, depending upon the various dispositions and inclinations of creatures of varied temperaments.

Parable of the Burning House[104]

According to this parable told to venerable Sāriputra by the Buddha, in a certain village there was a rich man having many children. One day his house was engulfed by a mass of fire. Having escaped himself from the fire, the rich man saw that his children were immersed in play and did not notice the fire. As their well-wisher he warned them several times to come out but they turned a deaf ear due to ignorance. In other words they did not understand the purport of the word "burning." Their father abundantly grieved and having contemplated many possibilities to rescue them at last having known the children's disposition promised them precious, admirable bullock-carts, deer-carts, and goat-carts if they come out of the burning house. Having been tempted by their father's promise the children ran out from the burning house and demanded for the toys. With a delighted heart their rich father gave to all of them real swift bullock-carts made up of precious substances and wonderful jewellery.

---

104. H. Kern (tr.), *op. cit.*, pp. 72-82.

Now the Buddha questions venerable Sāriputra whether the father should feel guilty of a falsehood and Sāriputra replied in negative. Because the father in the first instance as a guardian of the children has obligation to rescue his ignorant children from the danger. In order to achieve this end he can resort to some device to save them. Hence he has no other motto or object except the children's welfare. Similarly the Buddha of the *Lotus Sūtra* explains the philosophical significance of the parable as follows: Like the father of the burning house the Tathāgatha is free from all dangers. The dilapidated house in the parable is compared to the phenomenal existence or *saṁsāra*. The children are the sentient beings. Like the father in the parable, the Buddha is the father of the world who has highest perfection in skilful means, benevolent and compassionate. Through his skilful means the Buddha delivers the suffering beings from birth and death, pain and ignorance and brings them to supreme enlightenment.[105] Like the father in the parable who saved the children from the fire, the Buddha endeavours towards the emancipation of all sentient beings through three vehicles namely the Vehicle of Disciples, of Pratyeka Buddhas and that of Bodhisattvas, which are metaphorically referred in the parable as the goat-carts, deer-carts and bullock-carts. Like the rich father in the parable, the Buddha did not teach a particular *nirvāṇa* to each and every being. He shows the best of all ways or goals, i.e., known as *sarvajñatā*. It is known as the complete *nirvāṇa*.

Parable of the Prodigal Son[106]

A certain person went away from his father to some foreign parts of a country in search of livelihood. His father shifted himself to another distant place and in course of time turned

---

105. *Ibid.*, p. 82.

106. *Ibid.*, pp. 99-108.

out to be a rich man and his son who had left him long ago remained to be a poor fellow. After several years the poor son in quest of food and clothing wandering through villages, towns and provinces happened to reach the place where his father was dwelling in great pomp. The rich father was already longing for his son since he has no other blood-heir to enjoy his properties. Meanwhile his poor son approached the very house of his father who sat in a large assembly of elders. The father recognized his son but the latter could not recognize his father and he thought that he was a rich man or a king. The man having been frightened thought that he has no place to stay except to beg food and clothing and departed from that place. His rich father sent his assistants and fetched his son back and made arrangements secretly to employ him as his servant and began to supervise the performance of the poor man. Later, the father appeared in a shabby disguise before his son who was employed as a servant and encouraged him to work efficiently promising him to give whatever he wants such as extra pay, domestic requirements etc. After sometime the householder fell sick. He is satisfied with the poor man's efficiency in his duties and character. He called the poor man and told him to take hold off all responsibilities of managing his affairs and warned him to be careful. His poor son accepted the abundant treasures with great detachment and indifference and continued to live in the same hovel of straw and considered himself the same poor man as before. In course of time the poor man learnt the skill in management, value of labour and got himself mentally matured. After acknowledging his son's ability the rich man was contented. At the time of his death the rich man in the presence of the gathering of his relatives and citizens announced that the young man was nobody else but his lost son fifty years ago and narrated their blood relation. He then made his son the legal heir to all his riches. Having listened to this astonishing truth the young man thought by himself as though he got the abundant riches unexpectedly.

The above parable exemplifies the truth that all beings are the lost sons of Tathāgatha. They are oppressed with three difficulties such as the difficulty of pain, the difficulty of conception and the difficulty of transition. The sentient beings are prompted by the Lord to ponder on numerous inferior laws similar to a heap of dirt. The Tathāgatha by skilful means appoints us as heirs to the knowledge of Tathāgatha without our knowledge of real inheritance to it because the Buddha promised the ultimate *nirvāṇa* as our fee.[107]

Although, the Tathāgatha by his skilful means knows the dispositions of all sentient beings, the beings infected by ignorance do not apprehend this fact. Hence, the Buddha reminds us of our inheritance and the relation of our son-ship to him. The sentient beings play a double role. Insofar as in the presence of Bodhisattvas, they are persons of low dispositions. At the same time we have to rise to the Buddha's enlightenment. Having obtained the enlightenment the sentient beings remain detached and indifferent to worldly things like the young man in the parable who did not care for the riches.

Parable of Plants[108]

Addressing venerable Mahakasyapa and other senior disciples Lord Buddha taught that the real qualities of Tathāgatha are innumerable and incalculable. The Tathāgatha is the Master King of the law. He knows the meaning of all laws, as he possesses the faculty of penetrating all laws. He possesses the highest perfection of wisdom and displays the knowledge with great diligence.

---

107. *Ibid.*, p. 107.

108. *Ibid.*, pp. 118-21.

Just as a big cloud encompassing the universe showers the rain over all the grasses, shrubs, herbs, trees of various species living together with different names everywhere and simultaneously various kinds of trees referred above suck the humid element from the water emitted by the great cloud according to their respective faculties. Rooted in one soil, having drenched by the water of the same essence these various families of plants each according to its own germ acquire their own developments and growth.

Similarly, the Tathāgatha appears and sends forth the *dharma* to the whole world including gods and demons. By perfect wisdom the Tathāgatha knows the world as well as the next world. He is all-knowing and all-seeing. The Tathāgatha by his skilful means (*upāyakauśalya*), is acquainted with the path and different faculties and energies of beings. He inspects them and pleases them by means of tales, amusements, etc. so that in the latter world also they will find peace. By listening to the law the beings will be freed from hindrances and apply the knowledge according to power and strength to attain *nirvāṇa*. In the above parable the great cloud is a metaphor that represents the Buddha. The rain poured on the trees, etc., is the law preached by him to all beings. The essence of law is deliverance, annihilation, all-knowingness. The Buddha finally tells his disciples that after seeing the states of different beings from the lowest to highest without discrimination he delivers the same essence of *dharma*,[109] which will enable them to reach the goal of *nirvāṇa*.

Parable of Blind man and the Physician[110]

There lives a blind man who apparently has no visual differentiation of shape, colour, etc. He refuses to believe the

---

109. *Ibid.*, p. 121.

110. *Ibid.*, pp. 129-36.

existence of things of phenomenal existence owing to lack of his sight. A physician who knows all diseases by his skilful means thought a device and he applied some herbs (which he found after a long search in Himālayas), to the blind person who consequently acquired the eye-sight. Having gained the eyesight marvelling at the beauty of the world he was struck in wonder. He realized how foolish he was and he denied the existence of the phenomena. He began to claim that he is able to see every thing. Then the seers of five transcendent faculties warned him that he has not yet gained wisdom owing to the limitation of sense-organs. He ignorantly takes darkness for light and light for darkness. They advised the person who has gained the eyesight to be an ascetic abstaining from passions in order to acquire transcendental faculties. Following their advice the person becomes an ascetic. After obtaining perfection he grieved for his former ignorance, which shrouded his senses.

The moral taught by the Buddha in the parable is that the blind person is a metaphor for all ignorant creatures who struggle in the whirlpool of the worldly passions, owing to their ignorance of the law. The great physician in the parable is the Tathāgatha. The seers in the parable are the bodhisattavas. The four herbs prescribed by the physician in the parable are void-ness, causeless-ness, unfixed-ness and reaching *nirvāṇa*. The Buddha through innumerable means liberates the world-bound sentient beings similar to the physician of the parable[111] who cured the eyesight of the blind person.

Parable of Physician and his sons[112]

The Buddha narrates another parable, which is as follows: An intelligent and efficient physician has many sons. When he is

111. *Ibid.*, pp. 134-35.

112. *Ibid.*, pp. 304-06.

abroad his children suffer a disease from poison. Some of his children have perverted notions and others have right notions but all of them suffered in the same manner. On the arrival of back home the physician listens to their complaint with great affection. Then he prepares a drug as a remedy for poison and assured them that they will recover and will be healthy if they use the medicine. Those who had right notions quickly took the medicine and have been delivered from the ailment. But those children who have perverted notions refused to take the medicine. Then he thought of another device to save his perverted children. He told them that he is nearing death and showed the medicine once again to his children. The physician skilfully departed to another distant land and managed to make his children believe that he has expired. In grief and sorrow on their father's death and fully realizing their orphanage their minds turned to right notions. Then they instantly took the medicine and got freed from their disease. After knowing his children's recovery the physician appeared before them again.

There is no falsehood on the part of the physician since he was displaying skilful methods to deliver his children from the disease. In the same manner the Buddha concludes as a compassionate father of all sentient beings he resorts to various techniques to relieve the ignorant beings from their owes of existence and to lead them to the goal of perfect enlightenment.[113]

Thus, the Buddha of the *Saddharma Puṇḍarīka* affirms that he is the Tathāgatha, the transcendental sublime being endowed with unlimited span of life, glorious power, wisdom and infinitude of action. He proclaims himself as the self-born who appears in the world out of his own wish. He is also

113. *Ibid.*, pp. 306, 309-10.

depicted as the universal father, healer and protector of all beings. He is also the king, Lord and Master of all laws. His birth, efforts to attain enlightenment and his entering *Parinirvāṇa* are only skill-in-means to educate beings enabling them to realise the Tathāgatha knowledge.

Bibliography

Abeynayake, Oliver, *A Textual and Historical Analysis of the Khuddaka Nikāya*, Colombo, 1984.

Adhikari, R.B, "Khuddaka-Nikāya," *Encyclopedia of Buddhism*, vol. VI, Fasc. 2, Govt. of Srilanka, 1999.

Alexander Cosma De Koros, *The Life and Teachings of Buddha*, Calcutta, 1957.

Andre, Bareau, *Bouddha*, Seghers, Paris.

Barua, D.K., *An Analytical Study of Four Nikāyas*, Calcutta: Rabindra Bharati University, 1971.

Barua, D.L., *Elements of Pāli Grammar*, Calcutta: West Bengal Board of Secondary Education, 1968.

Beal, Samuel, *The Romantic Legend of Śākya Buddha*, London, 1875.

———, (tr.) *Dhammapada with accompanying Narratives* (*translated from the Chinese*), Calcutta: Susil Gupta (India) Ltd., 1952.

Bond, G.D., "Theravāda Buddhism and the Aims of Buddhist Studies," in A.K. Narain, (ed.) *Studies in History of Buddhism*, Delhi, 1980.

Buddharakshita, Acharya, *Concise Pāli Course*, Parts I & II, Bangalore: Buddhavacana Trust, 1978.

Bunno, Kato, Yoshiro Tamura and Kojiro Miyasaka (tr.), *The Threefold Lotus Sūtra with revisions* by W.E. Soothill, Wilhelm Schiffer and Pier P. Delcampana, New York: Weather Hill, Tokyo: Keck, 1975.

Childers, Robert Caesar, *A Dictionary of the Pāli Language*, Kyoto: Rinsen Book Co., 1976.

Conze, Edward, "The Diamond Sūtra and the Heart Sūtra," in the *Buddhist Wisdom Books*, London: George Allen and Unwin Ltd., 1958; 1970 third Imp.

———, *The Prajñāpāramitā Literature*, The Hague: Mouton & Co. Gravenhage, 1960.

———, "Mahāyāna Buddhism," in *Thirty Years of Buddhist Studies*, Oxford: Cassirer, 1967.

———, "Recent Progress in Buddhist Studies," in *Thirty Years of Buddhist Studies*, Oxford, 1967.

Dhammajoti, U., (tr.), *The Dhammapada*, Allahabad: Kitab Mahal, 1948.

Edgerton, Franklin, *Buddhist Hybrid Sanskrit Language and Literature*, Varanasi: Banaras Hindu University, 1954.

Fausboll, V., (tr.), *The Sutta-Nipāta*, SBE. vol. X, Delhi: Motilal Banarasidass, 1968.

Foucher, A., *The Life of Buddha according to the Ancient Texts and Monuments of India*, Wesleyan University Press, 1963.

Fujita, Kotatsu, *One Vehicle or Three, Journal of Indian Philosophy* 3, Dordrecht-Holland: D. Reidel Pub. Co., 1975.

Geiger, Wielhelm, *Pāli Literature and Language*, tr. into English by B. Ghosh, Calcutta: University of Calcutta, 1943.

Gemmel, William, (tr.), *The Diamond Sūtra* (*Chin-kang Ching*) or *Prajñapāramitā* (London: Kegan Paul, 1912; New York: E.P. Dutton & Co., 1913)

Goyal, S.R., *A History of Indian Buddhism*, Meerut: Kusumanjali Prakashan, 1987.

Hare, E.M., *Woven Cadences of Early Buddhists*, London: 1945, 1947.

Humphreys, Christmas, *The Buddhist Way of Life*, London: George Allen & Unwin Ltd., 1969.

———, *Buddhism*, Penguin Books, 1971.

———, *A Popular Dictionary of Buddhism*, London: Curzon Press, 1976.

Hurvitz, Leon, (trd.), *Scripture of the Lotus Blossom of the Fine Dharma*, Translated from the Chinese of Kumārajiva, New York: Columbia University Press, 1976.

Ikeda, Daisaku, *Buddhism in the First Millennium.* Translated By Burton Watson, Tokyo, New York and San Francisco: Kodansha International Ltd., Second Reprint, 1978.

Irving, Babbit, (trd.), *The Dhammapada,* New York: Oxford University Press, 1936.

Jagadish, Kashyap Bhikṣu, *Pāli Mahāvyākaran,* Delhi: Motilal Banarasidass, 1985.

Jaspers, Karl, *The Great Philosophers,* ed. By Hannah Arendt, Trd. Ralph Manheim, London: Rupert Hart-Davis, 1962.

Jennings, J.G., *The Vedāntic Buddhism of the Buddha,* London: Oxford University Press, 1949.

Joshi, L.M., *Studies in the Buddhistic Culture of India,* Delhi: Motilal Banarasidass, Second rev. edn, 1977.

———, (ed. and tr.) *Vajracchedikā Prajñapāramitā Sūtra with the Commentary of Asaṅga,* ed. By Samdhong Rinpoche, Sarnath: Central Institute of Higher Tibetan Studies, 1978.

Karunes, B., "Teachings of the Dhammapada," in *Journal of the Ganganatha Jha Research Institute,* Aug, 1951.

Kern, H., and Nanjio, B., *Saddharmapuṇḍarīka,* St. Petersburg: Bibliotheca Buddhica xii, 1912.

Kern, H., (tr.), *The Saddharmapuṇḍarīka or the Lotus of the True Law,* SBE, vol. XXI, Delhi: Motilal Banarasidass. 1968.

Kogen, Mizuno, "Dhammapada of various Buddhist Schools" in A.K. Narain (ed.), *Studies in Pāli and Buddhism,* Delhi: B.R. Publishing Corporation, 1979.

Law, Bimla Churn, *A History of Pāli Literature,* vol. I., Varanasi: Bharatiya Publishing House, 1937.

Law, B.C., "Some thoughts on the Buddhist Dhammapada," Bombay: *The Āryan Path,* vol. XXXIV, No. 3, March 1965.

Lord, Chalmers, (tr.) *Buddha's Teachings Being the Sutta-Nipāta* or *Discourse-Collection,* Harvard Oriental Series, vol. 37, 1932.

Malalasekera, G.P., "Some aspects of Reality as taught by Theravāda Buddhism" in C.A. Moore (ed.) *The Indian Mind,* Honolulu: University of Hawaii, 1967.

Martin, T.P., "The Saddharmapuṇḍarīka," in *Buddhism in England,* vol. VII, No. 2. July-August, 1932.

Max Müller, F., (trd.), *The Dhammapada*, SBE vol. X, Delhi: Motilal Banarasidass, 1977.

———, (tr.), *The Vajracchedika in Buddhist Mahāyāna Texts*, SBE vol. XLIX, part- II, Delhi: Motilal Banarasidass, 1978 reprint.

Nakamura, Hajime, *Gautama Buddha*, Tokyo: Los Angeles: Buddhist Books International, 1977.

———, *Indian Buddhism: A Survey with Bibliographical Notes*, Delhi: Motilal Banarasidass, 1987.

Nalinaksha, Dutt, *Saddharma Puṇḍarīka Sūtram,* with Mironov's Readings from Central Asian Mss., Calcutta: The Asiatic Society, 1953.

Narada, Mahathea, (tr.) *The Dhāmmapada*, Colombo: Vajirarama, Calcutta: Maha Bodhi Society, 1991.

———, *A Comprehensive Manual of Abhidhamma by Bhikkhu Bodhi*, Kandy, Sri Lanka: Buddhist Publication Society, 1993.

Naresh, Mantri, *The Lotus Sūtra, A New Interpretation*, Tokyo: Hokke Journal Co. Ltd., 1977.

Nikyo, Niwano, *Buddhism for Today* (*A Modern Interpretation of the Threefold Lotus Sūtra*). Tokyo: Kosei Pvt. Co, 1979.

Nyana Tiloka Mahathera, *Guide through the Abhidhamma Piṭaka*, Kandy, Sri Lanka: Buddhist Publication Society, 1983.

Oldenberg, H., *Buddha, His Life, His Doctrine, His Order,* Varanasi: Indological Book House, 1971.

Pande, G.C., *Studies in Mahāyāna*, Varanasi: Central Institute of Higher Tibetan Studies, Sarnath, 1993.

Pandey, Ramavadh, and Mishra, Ravinath, *Pāli-Vyakaran,* Delhi: Motilal Banarasidass, 1977.

Potter, Karl H., (ed.), *Encyclopaedia of Indian Philosophies,* vol VIII: Buddhist Philosophies from 100 to 350 AD, Delhi: Motilal Banarasidass, reprint, 2002.

Poussin, L., De La Vallee, "Lotus of the True Law," James Hastings (ed.), E.R.E. Edinburgh: T&T Clark, 1966.

Price, A.F. (trd.) *The Jewel of Transcendental Wisdom*, London: Buddhist Society, 1947; (reprinted as the *Diamond Sūtra* in 1955).

Ramayana Prasad Dvivedi, *Bauddha Sanskṛta Kāvya Sameeksha*, Varanasi: Banaras Hindu University, 1976.

Rhys Davids, T.W., *Buddhism — Being a Sketch of the Life and Teachings of Gautama the Buddha*, London, 1877.

Rhys Davids, T.W., and Stede, William, *Pāli English Dictionary*, New Delhi: Oriental Books Reprint Corporation, 1975.

Rockhill, W.W., *The Life of the Buddha*, London, 1884.

Saibaba, V.V.S., "Saddharma Puṇḍarīka Sūtra — A Devotional Treatise," Japan: *Young East*, vol. I, no.4, Autumn, 1975.

———, "The ideal of Bodhisattva in Vajracchedīkā Prajñāpāramitā or the Diamond Cutter," Calcutta: *The Mahā Bodhi*, vol. 83, no. 10, Oct.-Dec., 1975,

———, "Nirvāṇa as described in Sutta Nipāta," Sri Lanka: *World Buddhism*, vol. XXIV, no. 11, June 1976.

———, "Dhammapadamu," Hyderabad, *Journal of Telugu Studies*, vol. 1, no. 1, March, 1988.

———, "Buddhist Concept of Peace with special reference to the Sutta Nipāta," Bodh Gaya: *Sambodhi*, vol. 1, no. 1, May 1990.

——— "The Concept of Peace in Buddhist Literature" in *Buddhism and Peace an Interdisciplinary Study*, Visakhapatnam: Andhra University, 1991.

———, "The Concept of 'Yāna' in Mahāyāna Buddhism with special reference to the Saddharma Puṇḍarīka Sūtra," Calcutta: *The Mahā Bodhi*, vol. 102, No. 3, May-June 1994.

Sangharakshita, Bhikshu, *A Survey of Buddhism*, Bangalore: The Indian Institute of World's Culture, 1957.

Saunders, K.J., *Gautama Buddha*, London: Oxford University Press, 1922.

Senchu, Murano, (trd.), *The Lotus Sūtra or the Sūtra of the Lotus Flower of the Wonderful Law*, Japan: Nichiren Shu, 1974.

Soothill, W.E., (tr.), *The Lotus of the Wonderful Law*, (abridged trs. from Kumarajiva's Chinese Translation) Oxford: Clarendon Press, 1930.

Sukumari, Bhattacharji, *Buddhist Hybrid Sanskrit Literature*, Calcutta: The Asiatic Society, 1992.

Suzuki, Beatrice L., *Mahāyāna Buddhism*, London: Allen and Unwin, 1959.

Takakusu, J., "Buddhism as a Philosophy of Thusness" in C.A. Moore (ed.), *The Indian Mind*, Honolulu, East-West Centre Press, 1967.

Thomas, E.J., *The History of Buddhist Thought*, London: Kegan Paul, Trench, Trubner, 1933.

———, *The Life of Buddha as Legend and History*, New York, 1927, London, 1949.

Thittila, U., "The Fundamental Principles of Theravāda Buddhism," in K.W. Morgan (ed.), *The Path of the Buddha*, New York: Ronald Press, 1956.

Upadhyay, Bharat Singh, *Pāli Sāhitya kā Itihās*, Prayag: Hindi Sahitya Sammelan, 1972.

Vaidya, Dr. P.L., (tr.), *Dhammapada*, Poona: The Oriental Book Agency, 1934.

Vaidya, P.L., (ed.), *Saddharma Puṇḍarīka Sūtra*, Darbangha: The Mithila Institute of P.G. Studies and Research in Sanskrit Learning, 1960.

Wagiswara, W.D.C., and Saunders, K.J., (tr.), *The Buddha's way of Virtue*, London: John Murray, 1927.

Ward, C.H.S. *Buddhism*, vol. II, *Mahāyāna*, London: The Epworth Press, 1952.

Winternitz, Maurice, *A History of Indian Literature*, vol. II, New Delhi: Munshiram Monoharlal, 1977.

Woodward, F.L., (tr.), *The Buddha's Path of Virtue*, London, 1921.

Yamaguchi, S., "Development of Mahāyāna Buddhist Beliefs" in K.W. Morgan (ed.), *The Path of the Buddha*, New York: The Ronald Press, 1956.

Zaehner, R.C., (tr.), *The Bhagavad-Gītā*, London: Oxford University Press, 1973; Reprint, 1981.

Zimmer, Heinrich, *Philosophers of India*, ed. By Joseph Campbell, London: Routledge and Kegan Paul Ltd., 1953.

Index of Pāli and Sanskrit Works

Index of Technical Terms and Proper Names